HEADSHIP
MATTERS

Nicki Bell and Alistair Shaw

First Published 2024
Cadogan Press

© **2024 Nicki Bell and Alistair Shaw**

ISBN: 978-1-8380073-7-9

Set and designed by Cadogan Press
Printed by Book Printing UK

We dedicate this book to all the headteachers we have worked with, and continue to work with, who are committed to improving the lives of thousands of pupils across the country.

Keep up the great work!

ABOUT THE AUTHORS

Nicki Bell

My teaching career began in 1983 in Birmingham. I subsequently worked in Derbyshire, Norfolk and Suffolk and was headteacher of four primary schools over a period of twenty years. My final headship was in Sutton Coldfield in Birmingham before retiring in 2016. Prior to my final headship, I worked for four years for the eastern affiliated centre of the National College for School Leadership. I now support headteachers and senior leaders both in their schools and at training events, frequently working with Alistair.

Alistair Shaw

As a former primary headteacher of three substantive and one interim headships, I now enjoy my role in providing independent consultancy support and challenge to leaders at all levels in a wide range of contexts. I am former School Improvement Partner (SIP) across four Local Authority areas, Ofsted, and Diocesan Inspector. I was also an Associate at the National College for many years. I continue to facilitate and lead the review of headteachers' performance across many parts of the country.

Contents

Headship Matters

Maintaining focus on strategic direction

Managing the day-to-day operational tasks

Block 1: Personal values and beliefs
Know yourself; your values; your beliefs; your strengths and your weaknesses. Decide/agree on what are your 'go to the wall' motivations that underpin your leadership.

Block 2: Quality of teaching and learning
Have an embedded system to measure the quality of teaching over time fairly, consistently, and transparently. This enables teachers to recognise their own strengths and areas of development.

Block 3: Subject leadership
Build a team of strong subject leaders able to develop your curriculum; to lead others and to identify strengths and areas of improvement. Invest in continued professional development and succession planning.

Block 4: Performance management
Have systems in place to manage performance and give staff opportunities for professional development. Establish robust continued professional development programmes.

Block 5: Coaching and mentoring
Establish a coaching and mentoring culture as a powerful mechanism to enhance staff development. Staff develop effective coaching skills which support their individual professional development.

Block 6: Team culture
Be proactive in developing a culture of the highest expectations and excellence. Regularly revisit this. Know the strengths and development areas of your team.

Block 7: Governance
Work with your governing body to ensure that they have a solid understanding of their three core functions. Ensure governors receive regular training so that they can have a positive impact upon the school.

Block 8: Communication and well-being
Be consistent, fair, and honest. Make sure everyone knows and buys into the vision and values of the school. Look after yourself and your team. Work hard but make sure there is a work/life balance for everyone.

Block 9: Using and applying theory.
Keep abreast of relevant publications and information that can positively impact upon your school but don't jump on band wagons. Remember that context is everything in initiating new ideas.

Solid foundations: systems, processes, and consistency
These areas underpin all aspects of effective headship. You need to develop effective systems and processes to manage the bureaucracy of the school and then implement these in a consistent manner. This will enable you to be effective in your auditing, monitoring and evaluation of strengths and areas of development, resulting in effective school improvement.

Foreword

The role of headteacher is at once both enormously rewarding and unbelievably challenging. Most of the time it feels like the best job in the world, full of purpose, delight and wonderful surprises. But it can feel overwhelming, with the burden of expectations weighing heavy.

This book celebrates the good times as well as providing an absolute treasure trove of ideas and resources that will give heads the confidence to grow as leaders as well as saving them and their colleagues huge amounts of time in not having to reinvent the wheel.

Unlike most books, this handbook references over one hundred online resources available to download for a small one-off subscription that have been created and curated by two experienced and highly successful former headteachers.

Whether it be a template for improvement planning, a PowerPoint on the role of a subject leader or a lesson observation proforma using Rosenshine's principles of instruction, you will be hard pushed to come up with something that has not been included in this wide-ranging resource

I hope you enjoy reading the book and immersing yourself in the treasure trove of resources it references.

Andy Buck
Idridgehay

Introduction

Making the most of Headship Matters

We have written this book and created the resource bank as our legacy to the education system, in response to many requests from headteachers with whom we currently work.

From our collective experience of seven substantive headships and one interim headship, and from our extensive work with serving headteachers, we know and understand the demands headteachers continue to face in an ever more challenging and evolving system. Our careers also include; undertaking Ofsted and denominational inspections; supporting school leaders pre and post inspections; facilitating hundreds of headteacher appraisals as external advisers; working within the National College for School Leadership and Department for Education; independent leadership training and support for governors; writing and facilitating professional development programmes for leaders at all levels; and the development and marketing of products and resources for school leaders.

Over several years we have designed and created many resources for headteachers with the dual intent of supporting them in resolving their challenges, and providing robust and efficient systems that we know work consistently well. We hope that by now bringing these altogether into one place, they provide current and future headteachers with a rich-collection of materials intended to make their work easier.

Within this book you will find many of these resources referenced and extracts provided, together with underpinning rationales for their use and application. All the resources and materials have been created in Word, Excel or PowerPoint formats, and therefore can all be easily adapted to suit individual school contexts.

To access **all the resources** in the **online resource bank** for a small one-off subscription you can:

- ∞ email headshipmatters@proton.me or
- ∞ visit www.tinyurl.com/3vtzknpu or
- ∞ scan the QR code below

Upon payment of the subsequent invoice, you will receive your unique access arrangements to the resource bank including the link to ensure that the materials can only be accessed by authorised individuals.

Finally, we are enormously grateful to all the colleagues who have supported us in this process. Thanks go to Andy Buck for giving us the green light to proceed with this venture, and for publishing our book. Thanks also to Ken Monkman for being an excellent proof-reader. Without his attention to detail and suggestions for improvements, this book would not have reached the standard it has. We are also very grateful to the serving headteachers with whom we work, both individually and collectively, who have provided us with very positive words of encouragement to complete this project.

But most praise and thanks go to our respective spouses, Lindsay and Roger, for putting up with the countless conversations we have engaged them in throughout the writing process. Their enduring patience, love, and guidance has enabled us to complete this work in an efficient and enthusiastic manner.

Thank you all,

Nicki and Alistair

Foundations Stones

Systems and processes

 **WHY**

We have always believed that there are two fundamental areas that effective headteachers must have as strengths.

The first is access to a range of systems and processes that support them in managing the huge number of bureaucratic tasks that headteachers must complete.

The second is the ability to communicate effectively with colleagues, pupils, parents, external professionals, and the wider school community.

This foundation is the basis of the other building blocks. Headteachers may create these for themselves or may access commercially produced resources to help them. Creating these resources is incredibly time consuming and so, for many headteachers buying in resources and then adapting them to their own context is a good option. Our resources are all created in Word, Excel or PowerPoint so can be easily adapted.

Self-evaluation and school improvement planning drives school improvement. It is not done for Ofsted. Its purpose is to ensure that strategic leadership energy is focused on the things that matter. However, in the information that schools must provide by 8am on the day of inspection, in the current School Inspection Handbook, it includes 'strategic documents about the school, including a summary of any self-evaluation or equivalent'.

Within our nine building blocks model, the balance at the top, (in the roof), shows the need to focus on both the day-to-day operational tasks whilst maintaining a focus on the strategic direction for the school.

Both are of vital importance and effective headteachers ensure that time is spent in both domains. There are times when the operational must dominate, but headteachers need to be sufficiently self-disciplined to set aside time for the strategic work, as this is what drives school improvement.

Most headteachers with whom we work, found that the realities of managing the Covid period in schools required almost 100% of their time to be given to operational tasks. Once that period had passed, they were very aware of the need to get back to their strategic leadership as without this, schools would stand still.

Stoll and Fink said in 1996 that "schools are either getting better or getting worse, because the rapidly escalating pace of change makes standing still impossible." Nearly thirty years later, if anything, the pace of change is even faster.

Three key elements of the strategic leadership cycle are school self-evaluation, school improvement planning and a comprehensive monitoring plan.

For many years we have been supporting school leaders in carrying out effective self-evaluation which has then directly informed the next stages of school improvement planning which in turn has been the basis of the monitoring plan.

Our strategic leadership cycle (resource bank reference 1)

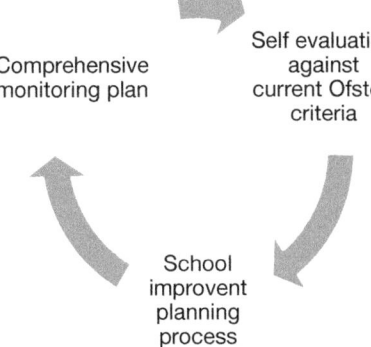

Including lesson visits; book/marking scrutiny; pupil progress meetings; data analysis; pupil voice, external verification

Comprehensive monitoring plan

Self evaluation against current Ofsted criteria

Including self-evaluation at different levels e.g. whole school, subject, phase or focus area e.g. SEND.

School improvent planning process

1. Overview
2. Action plans

The School Evaluation Form, (SEF), and School Improvement Plan, (SIP), are intended as tools, to be used very regularly by school leaders as they work to drive improvement. To be effective, self-evaluation must be robust, honest, and regularly revisited. Done well, it gives a picture of both the strengths and the current areas of development for the school. It is a process that drives school improvement by identifying the next steps to be acted upon.

We believe that the school improvement plan must be precisely drawn from the self-evaluation process. When working with headteachers we highlight identified areas for improvement in the SEF and lift them straight into the SIP. It seems logical to us, that a robust SEF should clearly identify the next steps of improvement for the school.

Self-evaluation

What does the SEF need to contain?

The first step in self-evaluation is to establish exactly what you need to evaluate. Whilst the process is not primarily for Ofsted, it seems sensible to use the five current areas of judgement, as schools are accountable for these when the inspectors visit.

Many models of SEF writing are available. We have developed a SEF template (resource bank reference 2), with two sections. Section A contains information about the context of the school; the progress against previous Ofsted issues and the areas identified on the school improvement plan. Section B is where we evaluate the five Ofsted judgement areas and the overall effectiveness of the school.

In our model, we have crafted the questions in each section to capture the essential elements that need to be evaluated. There are fifty-one questions in total, of which eleven relate to the Early Years Foundation Stage, (EYFS). Each question is evaluated and evidence to support the self-evaluation is identified. At the end of each of the five judgement areas, action points are identified which are then transferred directly to the school improvement plan, (SIP).

Evaluation rather than description (resource bank reference 3)

Our experience when working with school leaders, is that the natural tendency is to describe what is happening in school, rather than evaluating it. For example:

Quality of education question:

Teachers present subject matter clearly, promoting appropriate discussion about the subject matter being taught. They check pupils' understanding systematically, identify misconceptions accurately and provide clear, direct feedback. In so doing they respond and adapt their teaching as necessary without unnecessarily elaborate or individualised approaches.

An evaluative response:
∞ Continuous and rigorous monitoring, (lesson visits, workbook scrutinies, discussions with pupils), drives improvements to teaching, learning and assessment. We know this is making a sustained difference as all teaching is now good, and much is consistently better than good, having eradicated less than good teaching.
∞ Areas for improvement are immediately identified and structured and intensive support is provided to ensure highest standards of teaching. The result of this is consistency in the quality of provision across all subjects.

A descriptive response:
- ∞ Observations are undertaken by the headteacher and deputy headteacher.
- ∞ Work scrutiny is conducted by each subject leader.
- ∞ Monitoring and feedback are provided verbally for the teacher to respond to.
- ∞ Progress and attainment data is gathered three times a year for core subjects and once a year for foundation subjects.

It is important that school leaders focus on the evaluative responses as the descriptive ones will not necessarily identify the areas for improvement. Our resource bank contains a guidance booklet with evaluative questions to help complete each section and suggested evidence to support judgements, (resource bank reference 4). For example:

Intent: 1. How is the school curriculum designed to ensure that it is ambitious, coherently planned and sequenced toward cumulatively sufficient knowledge and skills and is taught in a logical progression, systematically and explicitly enough for all pupils to acquire the intended knowledge and skills for future learning?
Evaluation questions: Outline the principles underpinning your school curriculum design and implementation. Indicate how it was designed to meet the needs of your children in your context. How is it designed to build knowledge and skills? Is the curriculum planned to enable pupils to build knowledge and skills towards defined end points? What is unique/special about your school curriculum? How frequently is this evaluated to ensure that it meets the needs of pupils at all ability levels? To what extent is the curriculum being delivered in line with statutory requirements (if appropriate)? Are any schemes used, adapted to meet the needs of the children/context of the school? If so, how were schemes selected? Why were they needed? To what extent is the teaching of basic skills enhanced through foundation subjects – provide brief examples. **Evidence:** Curriculum Intent statements; curriculum map; curriculum planning; work scrutinies; peer to peer review outcomes; website – individual year group curriculum; planning; children's books; school environment; subject leader's folders and action plans; monitoring cycle of curriculum review; staff professional development log; pupil outcomes

A further way to support school leaders in writing in an evaluative way, rather than simply describing activities is to use sentence starters that generate an evaluative response. For example, if a sentence starts with a phrase such as "One example of effectiveness in this area is …." or, "Monitoring of this area shows that …." this will lead into evaluation of the issue in the question, (resource bank reference 5).

Within the response to each question, we add in signposting to evidence. The purpose of this is so that anyone, reading the SEF, can see how the response was created and interrogate the evidence that supports the judgement. Our intention is that this is not collated, but simply identified.

The school improvement plan (SIP)

We always reference this as an "improvement" plan, not a "development" plan. Our logic is that developments are on-going areas that would happen anyway such as playground re-surfacing. Improvements are those strategic issues that are going to make a real difference to the school, for example, through pupil outcomes and the quality of provision across the school.

If self-evaluation is effective, it must directly inform the SIP – issues in the SIP must come from the SEF. Our suggestion is that when improvement areas are identified whilst writing the SEF, that these are highlighted and immediately transferred to Section A4 – 'key areas identified for improvement'. The issues identified on the SIP may have different time frames. There may be issues that will be addressed within a term; equally there may be some longer-term issues – both are fine. Strategic improvements do not fit neatly into an annual plan and throughout the year, when the SEF is reviewed, new issues may arise, and these can be added to the SIP.

Our SIP is very simple. There are three non-negotiables that must be answered before an issue can be put on the SIP.

1. Do you have a compelling reason for the improvement?
    Without this there may be resistance to the change. Why would your team want to spend time and effort if it doesn't understand why you want to initiate this change?

2.   Can you identify the clear vision of the future i.e. the impact of the change?
     If the team doesn't know what it is you are trying to achieve, leaders may well be confused about the direction of travel.

3.   Do you have a coherent action plan identifying the steps needed?
     If the team doesn't know what you want members to do, then they can't support the change.

Our suggestion is that you capture the issues on a school improvement plan single sheet to display your school improvement actions for the year. This can be shared with anyone needing an overview of your priorities for the year, including governors. The overview SIP does not need to have actions in each of the five Ofsted areas, unless these have emerged from the SEF, (resource bank references 6 and 7). For example, if your self-evaluation is that behaviour and attitudes are outstanding and there is no identified need to change anything during the year ahead, then there is no need to contrive improvement points. Focus on the important. This is an exercise in identifying genuine priorities, not creating additional work. The size of the plan does not relate to the effectiveness of it.

The next step is to complete a more detailed plan for each of the identified improvement areas using the template, (resource bank references 8 and 9). The template references the three non-negotiables:

∞ What is the issue – the compelling reason?
∞ What differences are we intending to make – the impact of the change?
∞ The actions we will undertake to achieve the impact i.e. what, how, who, when and the cost – both financial and in terms of time.

Using this model, the SIP will not be overly large, but will be a working document that can be regularly annotated to update, probably on a termly basis. It is important that updating does not mean typing the whole plan again – handwritten annotations are quicker and demonstrate that it is a working document.

We would also suggest that the same proforma is used for subject improvement plans or any others specific area plans, such as SEND –

the model works just as well for these, although we would suggest no more than three to four action points for the year for subject plans.

 CASE-STUDY

"The SEF and SIP writing process are intrinsically linked, and each informs the other. We are fortunate to have worked with Nicki Bell as our school improvement consultant for several years. This has benefited the school in numerous ways, but regarding the SEF and SIP it has meant that Nicki has a thorough working knowledge of our school, (warts and all), which has enabled her to challenge and ask the right questions when working with our senior leadership team to write our SEF.

The opportunity for high quality, meaningful, professional dialogue as part of this evaluation process has enabled us to clearly identify the strengths of the school – as well as the specific areas requiring planned, strategic focus, i.e. our SIP. Through this collaborative evaluation and discussion, we identify the 'compelling reason for change', vital to the improvement process. In our experience, if we as leaders are transparent and honest about the need for change, and articulate this effectively with our staff, the improvement truly becomes a whole staff shared focus and the impact more powerful and sustained.

In our recent Ofsted inspection, our senior leaders felt more confident to articulate the evaluation and school improvement processes. Teachers, when asked about the school improvement focus areas, understood and were able to explain how and why these had been identified, supporting the inspectors in triangulating evidence. Whilst the Ofsted inspection is invariably a rigorous scrutiny of a school's practices, having worked through the school evaluation and improvement planning in this way certainly empowered our senior leaders to talk with confidence and accuracy about our school's strengths and weaknesses."

Alison Walklett
Head Teacher, New Oscott Primary School, Birmingham

 # CASE-STUDY

"Nicki and Alistair have designed an excellent, efficient, and evaluative process to complete a SEF which informs the SIP. This allows effective school improvement, ensuring school leaders have an accurate strategic view and plan for their school. The process is highly manageable and effective and would be highly recommended."

Ed Hobson
Head Teacher, St-Annes Primary School, Brown Edge, Staffordshire.

REFLECTIONS

∞ A robust and honest self-evaluation process, which identifies the key issues for the school improvement plan, will drive school improvement.

∞ Improvement plans are about focusing on the important next steps – not about capturing every possible improvement you can think of.

∞ SEFs and SIPs need to be widely shared and regularly reviewed – they won't help if once written they are stored in a filing cabinet.

∞ Have an annual cycle where the SEF and SIP are written together – our advice would be to allocate a full day in the second half of the summer term and get them completed so they are in place for the start of the new school year.

∞ Keep the writing team small – we might suggest headteacher and deputy headteacher. The wider team can then review before finalising the documents.

 # RESOURCES

Resource 1
Our strategic leadership cycle.

Resource 2
Blank SEF template.

Resource 3
Evaluation versus description.

Resource 4
A guide to SEF writing.

Resource 5
Fifty-five SEF phrases and statement starters.

Resource 6
A blank school improvement plan overview.

Resource 7
A sample SIP overview.

Resource 8
A blank template school improvement plan.

Resource 9
A sample SIP for leadership and management.

Resource 10
School self-evaluation evidence library – signposting to evidence.

Resource 11
The SEF and SIP explanatory notes.

Examples from the resource bank

Intent: 5. How do you develop the cultural capital needed to succeed in life? *'The essential knowledge that pupils need to be educated citizens'* (para: 250 SIH)
Evaluation questions: Curriculum map and points of revisiting/consolidation; how are you equipping pupils with cultural capital? External moderation – pupil voice **Evidence:** Lesson visits, work scrutiny, pupil interviews,

Implementation 2. Do teachers present subject matter clearly enabling all pupils to understand key concepts? How do teachers check pupils' understanding? How do they correct misunderstandings?
Evaluation questions: How effectively is prior learning used by teaching staff when assessing what pupils are capable of? What are leaders doing to ensure that this is rigorously applied in a consistent manner? How strong are questioning skills? Do teachers check pupils' understanding and identify and correct misconceptions? Are children able to respond to feedback independently so that this enables them to take next steps? How well do pupils' respond to feedback provided by teaching staff that demonstrates their learning? How do leaders know this? What do pupil's say when questioned about their feedback dialogue with teachers? Is there tangible evidence that this is happening in-line with the school's marking and feedback policies? To what extent are pupils provided with differentiated success criteria within each lesson that enables them to achieve and be appropriately challenged? **Evidence:** On-going assessment data. Work scrutiny. Teachers' planning, Teaching over time records

A writer's guide to drafting self-evaluation judgements with
supporting text - Resource bank reference 4.

School Self-Evaluation Evidence Library The intention is that this list signposts to <u>possible</u> different pieces of evidence that you use in your individual context. It is not intended that evidence is collated centrally nor that this is an exhaustive list – each school will have different systems and processes.

1. **Quality of Education**

   Curriculum intent, implementation, impact statements
   Curriculum maps; progression maps; knowledge organisers|
   Curriculum planning
   Model of learning process e.g. prior learning; logical sequence of teaching;
   defined end point
   Teaching over time records e.g. Records of work scrutiny, Records of lesson
   visits, evidence of application of teacher standards
   Questioning audit
   Moderation records
   Assessment processes
   Any examples of evidence-informed practice

A few examples from the evidence library
Resource bank reference 10

School Improvement Plan 2024-25
Based on self-evaluation priorities

Area 1: Quality of Education

Issue 1: To further develop ....

Issue 2: To review the provision of ....

Issue 3: To ensure that ......

Area 2: Behaviour and attitudes

Issue 1:

Area 3: Personal development

Issue 1

Area 4: Leadership and management

Issue 1:

Area 5: Early Years

Issue 1

A blank SIP overview
Resource bank reference 6

Sample school Improvement Plan 2023-24
Based on self-evaluation priorities

Area 1: Quality of Education

Issue 1: To refine the key knowledge that we want pupils to learn across the foundation subjects. To spend time deeply researching the fundamental skills and knowledge of the subjects and using professional judgement to review content across all key stages.

Issue 2: We are aware from our work on cognitive science, that the more explicit the links across subjects, the deeper the learning. We will therefore be reviewing this area to ensure that links are made where possible without contriving them artificially.

Issue 3: To support our Subject Leaders to enable them to write their own self-evaluation reports for their subjects. This will enable them to follow the school cycle of SEF; identification of improvements and then monitoring to measure impact.

Area 2: Behaviour and attitudes

Issue 1: To review our behaviour policy and introduce restorative practice alongside 'Marvellous Me' to promote individualised reward systems that encompass whole school values and attendance.

Area 3: Personal Development

Issue 1: To develop the Pupil Parliament which will include taking a group of children to Parliament to lobby our local MP.

Issue 2: To attain the Rights Respecting Schools Silver award (UNICEF) and develop the children's understanding of children's rights across the world.

Area 4: Leadership and management

Issue 1: Following inspection, we need to develop more robust monitoring processes to enable the SLT to measure consistency in the quality of teaching, assessment, and progress.

Issue 2: Inspection identified the need for Governors to hold school leaders to account to enable them to support the strategic direction of the school.

Area 5: Early Years

Issue 1: To improve communication and ensure parents have a clear understanding of what is expected of children and how to help them at home.

Issue 2: To ensure consistency in the quality of teaching and learning as a new team of staff develop in the EYFS.

A sample SIP overview containing the identified improvement areas
Resource bank reference 7

Effective Monitoring

 **WHY**

This section is designed to help you create a robust monitoring system, that ensures monitoring is an on-going process, measuring the things that need to be measured, rather than the things that can be measured, to support your school team in its drive for on-going improvement.

We recognise that school leaders are monitoring different aspects of their school.

We believe that having an overview of a generic model may help you to further develop your own context-specific monitoring strategy.

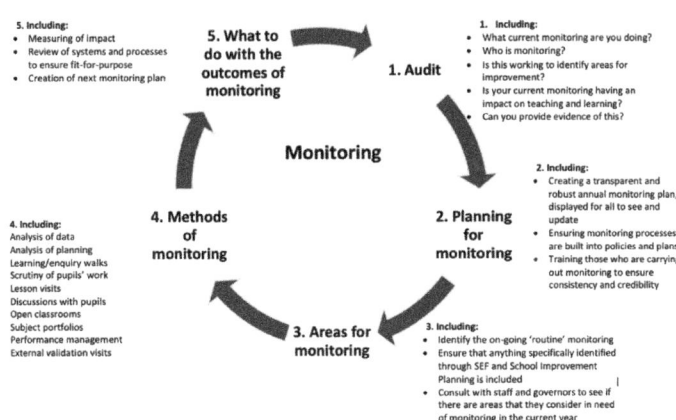

Our monitoring cycle
Resource bank reference 12

 **HOW**

Audit

As part of on-going self-evaluation, it is good practice to regularly audit systems and processes. The crux of auditing monitoring is to consider whether it is having a positive impact on teaching and learning, and, if this is the case, what evidence the school leaders have to prove this. With the myriad list of tasks to be completed in school, sometimes a plan that has worked well is simply rolled forward year-on-year without review, resulting in monitoring being a time-consuming, but not always a highly effective process.

The simplest audit would be to ask a series of questions of everyone involved in the process, for example:

∞ What monitoring is being done?
∞ Is it working to identify areas for improvement i.e. is there a link between monitoring and the school improvement plan or subject plans?
∞ Is there a tangible impact of monitoring on teaching and learning i.e. because of feedback on monitoring an area such as marking, does the specific focus improve?

Planning for monitoring

One of the most important school documents created every academic year is the monitoring plan. It is only of value if it is shared by all of those involved in it; is on display for them throughout the year and can be amended and updated by everyone involved e.g. when a task is completed or changed for any reason. A typical monitoring plan may look like this:

Sample Monitoring Timetable

Includes aspects associated with: Performance Management   Assessments   Quality of provision   Pupils   Parents   Systems

	Week 1	Week 2	Week 3	Week 4
Sept		Baselines Enquiry Walk	Lesson visits	SEF and SIP review/update
		School Council – pupil voice	Website check	External monitoring
Oct	Performance Management	Work scrutiny	Induction questionnaire	Half Term
			PPMs Review of interventions	
Nov	School Council – pupil voice	Enquiry Walk	Data analysis (national results)	
	Partner school moderation	Lesson visits	Work Scrutiny	Parent Interviews
Dec	Assessments, data drop 1	Attendance data PPMs	Enquiry Walk	Christmas break
	Website check. Parent workshops	Review of interventions		
Jan		Work Scrutiny	Lesson visits	Enquiry Walk
				SEF and SIP review/update
Feb	Mid-Year PM reviews	Pupil voice	Half Term	Review of interventions
	Annual parent questionnaire	External monitoring		
Mar	Assessments data drop 2	Enquiry Walk PPMs	Website check	Lesson visits
	Subjects review	Attendance data	Local schools' moderation	Parent Interviews
Apr	Work Scrutiny	Easter break		Review of interventions
	Parent workshops			

Resource bank reference 13

Areas for monitoring

This will depend upon the context of the school, but certain elements will be shared by all schools, for example, regular book scrutinies; pupil voice; pupil progress meetings; lesson visits/observations; data updates and reviews of subject portfolios.

One approach we use each time we work with a headteacher, and the senior leadership team is to ask them, individually, to complete the "One page school audit" see below, (resource bank reference 14). This is a very quick, 'spot in time' exercise, with each leader ticking the most appropriate box, according to their perception at that moment.

We then reveal our evaluations and look for similarities and differences. The next step is to explore the evidence underpinning those evaluations and what needs to be acted upon to facilitate improvement.

School Improvement Audit – Analysis of Priorities

Date completed:

Aspect/Focus	Red ✓	Amber ✓	Green ✓	Concerns/comments
Personal judgement of overall effectiveness				
Leadership				
SLT effectiveness				
Subject leader effectiveness				
Expectations and ambition for pupils				
Governance				
Monitoring - impact				
Culture and ethos				
Quality/impact of CPD				
Staff well-being/workload				

Sample section from one-page audit
Resource bank reference 14

The areas for monitoring should also link to the school improvement plan, if relevant. For example, if a focus on reading is in the SIP, then the monitoring activities related to that should be clearly referenced in the monitoring plan.

It is important that all of those who are involved in the monitoring processes are consulted and/or involved in creating the plan. There may well be areas of monitoring that the creators of the plan are unaware of but need to be included.

Methods of monitoring

There are many different methods, depending on the focus of the monitoring. These include analysing data and planning; carrying out a book scrutiny or lesson visits/observations; talking with pupils; eliciting information through questionnaires and audits through to formal external validation visits.

Each method will have its own protocols which have been created by leaders. For example, some schools run 'open classroom' sessions, when a wide range of monitoring tasks are completed in a fixed period-of-time. Other schools may be involved in regular external validation by other local headteachers or consultants.

 **CASE-STUDY**

What to do with the outcomes of monitoring

There must be an impact from monitoring, otherwise it becomes a bureaucratic process that takes significant time but does not support school improvement. Most aspects of monitoring, such as reading screening or a book scrutiny, are relatively easy to measure for impact. They measure a 'spot in time' and when re-visited, changes should be tangible. The resource entitled "Scrutinising pupils' work", (resource bank reference 16), provides guidance as to the most effective way to approach this activity to ensure only the most appropriate evidence is collected and acted upon.

There may be explicit follow-up from monitoring. For example, if when monitoring a specific subject, it becomes evident that there are issues around subject knowledge then some professional development will be necessary, the outcome of which should be an improvement as seen in the follow-up monitoring.

We are frequently asked by headteachers to undertake monitoring activities with key leaders. One such example involved Alistair in working with some subject leaders in a primary school to monitor and evaluate the quality of teaching and learning during mathematics lessons. Together, we visited lessons and talked with pupils. When observing teaching, it became clear that most teachers were only using one questioning strategy, namely that of asking a question and waiting for pupils to indicate their willingness to respond by having their hand up. This could mean that pupils who don't want to engage know to keep their hand down.

Furthermore, a clear gender bias began to emerge, with the boys being favoured to respond by a factor of 3:1, the evidence being a tally mark record being maintained as the lessons progressed. It is often the case that girls are underconfident in maths and therefore remain passive.

Feedback to the teachers whose lessons were visited contained two recommendations. One was that a wider questioning repertoire should be used by all teachers to maintain active pupil engagement. Secondly, teachers should be aware of equity to both genders when asking pupils to respond to questions. Professional development sessions were then provided to enable full understanding and implementation by all teachers.

Upon Alistair's return to the school the following term, visits to lessons revealed a full repertoire of questioning being used by all teachers with close attention being given to gender equity.

⛷ REFLECTIONS

∞ Establish clarity of purpose – the why of monitoring.
∞ Engage others fully in the process by providing training and support.

∞ Create a plan.

∞ Agree approaches to be used and by whom, within each aspect.

∞ Gather evidence for analysis, feedback and for creating a bias to action.

 # RESOURCES

Resource 12
Monitoring cycle diagram.

Resource 13
Sample monitoring timetables.

Resource 14
School improvement one page audit.

Resource 15
Monitoring form to evaluate the Mike Bell 5-stage learning cycle.

Resource 16
Scrutinising pupils' work – guidance.

Resource 17
A PowerPoint presentation on guidance for learning walks.

Resource 18
Guidance for undertaking learning/enquiry walks.

Resource 19
Effective learning environment flowchart.

Resource 20
Monitoring the learning environment – guidance.

Resource 21
Sample learning environment policy.

Examples from the resource bank

Monitoring form to evaluate the application of the 5-stage learning cycle.

Name of Teacher: Class: Date: Subject:

Learning cycle dimension	WHAT WE HOPE TO SEE	EVIDENCE
1.Prior Knowledge	• The teacher checking in-topic knowledge i.e. specific topic related information children have retained from earlier lessons or topics. • The teacher checking pre-topic knowledge – some of the basics that we might assume children know already.	
2.Presentation	• The teacher limiting new material – teaching small chunks of information. • The teacher explicitly helping children to make connections with learning in other subjects and links to prior knowledge.	
3.Challenge	• The teacher ensuring that tasks are not too easy or too hard. • Strategies used such as worked examples; modelling; dual coding (explaining the concept in different ways); giving time for reflection and collaborative working.	

Sample monitoring form
Resource bank reference 15

Scrutinising pupils' work – Guidance

Purpose

Work scrutiny can be used to:
• Evaluate learning and progress; standards of attainment; attitudes to work; typicality of teaching across the school and over time; curriculum coverage; adherence to school policies, (marking, calculation etc.)
• Identify the detail of the strengths and areas in need of improvement
• Evaluate the impact of actions taken to improve an area for improvement and the next steps to secure ongoing improvement

Sources of evidence which may prompt the need for a scrutiny of pupils' work:
• Data analysis
• Ofsted inspection
• Lesson observations
• LA/MAT review/Quality assurance visit
• Pupil feedback

Roles and responsibilities

Head Teacher and/or Senior Leaders:
• Identifies the focus and frequency
• Creates a monitoring schedule for the year
• Ensures subject leaders have clarity about their role in the process
• Builds in time for feedback from the monitoring activity
• Works with the subject leader(s) to ensure school/subject action planning reflects key areas identified for improvement. This will include detailing specific actions, with a short timeline, (no more than 6 weeks), an impact review and a report for staff and governors, as well as time to plan next actions.
• Feedback summary outcomes to staff and governors, including planned next steps.

Scrutinising pupils' work – guidance
Resource bank reference 16

Improving, (and proving), the quality of provision through learning/enquiry walks

Notes of guidance

Rationale for undertaking learning/enquiry walks:

Learning/enquiry walks are a key means of gathering evidence about the effectiveness of the school in a range of contexts. They are for professionals to lead the development of others, gather evidence about the quality of provision, over time and structure developmental feedback for others. Also, leaders can use learning/enquiry walks to inform other interested parties such as governors and parents.

This guidance is intended to help leaders structure, undertake and act upon the evidence generated from learning/enquiry walks, in order that provision for teaching and learning continues to improve. The analysis of outcomes can be included in your evidence portfolio/library to be shared with external agencies.

The templates are designed to aid leaders in:

1. Planning your walk, (including protocols)
2. Collecting data during the walk and
3. Reflecting on what your walk has taught you about the school.
4. Structuring feedback to others

Resource bank reference 18

Establishing an effective learning environment – flowchart
Resource bank reference 19

Monitoring the Learning Environment

The quality of the Learning Environment has a positive impact on the teaching and learning process. Leaders need to ensure that they have clear policies that are adhered to by all staff to ensure consistency and effectiveness throughout the school.

Four essential factors:
1.Ease of access by and for the learners within the classroom

* Easily understood, labelled and accessed resources to promote learner independence from adults
*Clearly differentiated workbooks etc. for subjects/areas of study
*Clear role and responsibilities within the learners' group of who fulfils roles such as distribution of books and resources etc.
*Instant access on worktables to essential equipment and frequently required resources.
*Easily viewed and referenced personal targets for learners.
*Learning protocols are understood and applied by all?
*All adults (including supply staff) follow established protocols and expectations.

Monitoring the learning environment – guidance
Resource bank reference 20

 **FURTHER READING**

Mike Bell, "The fundamentals of teaching" Routledge, 2021

Alex Bedford, "Pupil book study – an evidence informed guide to help quality assure the curriculum" John Catt Educational Ltd, 2021

Establishing consistency of provision and practice

 **WHY**

Establishing and embedding consistency across the school is potentially one of the greatest challenges faced by headteachers and school leaders. However, when achieved, it defines the distinctive character of your school which is plain for others to see.

Ofsted, (in an earlier framework), placed great emphasis on this factor as the essential difference between a 'good' and an 'outstanding' school. We believe there is still the compelling reason for taking the challenge of embedding a high degree of consistency.

With consistency come the following outcomes:
- ∞ Clarity for all,
- ∞ Coherence of understanding by all, and
- ∞ Confidence in all to take risks and contribute even more.

Without consistency come:
- ∞ Confusion,
- ∞ Anxiety, and
- ∞ Lack of commitment.

Why wouldn't you take up the challenge of establishing and embedding this for the lasting benefit of your pupils and staff?

 **HOW**

This resource is intended to help you progress down the pathway of embedding consistency. We have identified four key elements of consistency that enables anyone to see and feel it in daily practice. Within these four elements we have created some question prompts intended to help you reflect upon the current practice in your school.

Then, by using the audit grid you can identify the sequence of your actions to embed consistency even deeper.

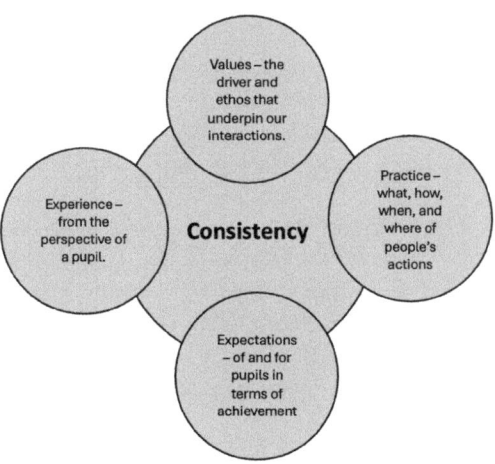

The four dimensions of consistency

Developing consistency across school

Consistency dimension	What might this include?	What actions would you take to develop this dimension?	What impact would you want this to have?
Consistency of practice: What people do How they do it and When and where they do it			
Consistency of experience: From a child's perspective, what do they experience as they move through the school?			
Consistency of expectation: In terms of pupil outcomes, uniformity of achievement from similar starting points			
Consistency of values: Living out in daily practice the ethos and values distinctive to the school Rhetoric into reality			

Resource bank reference 24

The first steps in establishing the principles of consistency

Consistency of Practice – to what extent is the…
Consistency of approach from SLT members evident to others across the school?
Deployment of staff transparent to all concerned.
Monitoring across the school compliant with agreed principles?
Planning completed by teaching staff understandable by others?
Marking of pupils' work and the monitoring of that marking the same for all teaching staff?
Learning environment largely the same as pupils progress through the school?
Pupil voice listened to and acted upon by decision makers?
Phase meeting leader fulfilling overall school policy and vision?
Records/Minutes of meetings reflective of the overall goals and intentions for the current academic year?

Resource bank reference 23

The full version of the first steps in establishing the principles of consistency can be found at resource bank reference 23.

You can use the slide set, contained within the resource bank reference 22 as a starter with groups of staff and/or governors and then engage these groups in auditing current practice followed by planning for action to either plug gaps or extend practice even further. It is the professional dialogue followed by actions that is the key to success with this.

Finally, we have included some scenarios for you to use with your senior leaders, to consider and discuss. These are intended to help you map out what should happen in specific circumstances.

This will lead to a closer degree of alignment across the leadership team and provide you as headteacher with assurance that responses in your absence by others will be of the same nature as if you were dealing with those situations yourself.

Examples of scenarios to use with your team within the slide set, (resource bank reference 22) are shared here.

> **Scenario 1:**
> Following a parent-teacher consultation the previous day, two parents were told that they child was making good progress and becoming in line with age related expectations. Parents demand an immediate appointment with you because they believe that their child is the most able child in the class. What do you do?

> **Scenario 2:**
> We have just appointed a new KS1 leader from another school who has already instructed teachers within her phase to demonstrate planning in a format that is not fit-for-purpose in our context. They have done this without any prior reference to the HT or DHT. What do you do?

 **CASE-STUDY**

Working with headteachers in schools, we are often requested to evaluate the extent of consistency across the school. In undertaking this evidence gathering process, we frequently start with the experience pupils gain as they move up through the school. Reducing the variability of pupils' experience, in terms of teachers' expectations will enable smooth transition from one class to another. A child having to adjust to a new set of expectations will inevitably have his/her learning inhibited in the early stages of the school year. The aim here is not have lots of "little schools within one" but to enable the transition period to be as short as possible.

Several schools we work with have adopted the practice of pupils working with their new teacher from mid-June to overcome the hiatus of the long summer break combined with the anxieties of the "new class in September" experience. What those teachers and headteachers tell us is that the start back in September is much smoother as expectations are known and learning can become embedded more quickly. Another useful strategy is for workbooks to be passed up with the pupils, so that they simply continue on the next page at the start of the new year. This enables teachers to ensure that expectations in areas such as presentation and stamina for learning are maintained.

When we look at the consistency of expectations, in more detail, we are focussed upon what adults do, how they do it, and when they do it. For example, is there coherence of understanding across the teaching team of what is expected in terms of achievement from pupils with different starting points?

Furthermore, is there clear evidence to secure teacher assessment processes and skills in order that teachers feel secure about judgements through moderation internally and working with other schools? Is there evidence that there is a clear assessment data system within the school which informs a detailed analysis of the relative achievement of key groups of pupils? Do pupil progress review meetings, (PPMs), result in consistent progress, identification of next steps and interventions for identified pupils?

Are pupils in receipt of consistent experiences in each class, as monitored by senior staff through a range of processes? Are the same messages and same training being provided for everyone across the teaching team? Do all staff understand and implement whole school expectations?

REFLECTIONS

∞ The four dimensions of consistency – values, practice, expectations, and pupils' experiences.
∞ Audit, monitor and develop practice.
∞ Induct new pupils and staff into "the way we do things around here".
∞ Revisit, remind, clarify, and repeat until you have consistency as a cornerstone of your school.

 # RESOURCES

Resource 22
A PowerPoint presentation to support the SLT in considering consistency.

Resource 23
The first steps in establishing consistency.

Resource 24
Proforma for developing the four dimensions of consistency.

To access **all the resources** in the **online resource bank** for a small one-off subscription just:

∞ email headshipmatters@proton.me or
∞ visit www.tinyurl.com/3vtzknpu or
∞ scan the QR code below

Focus on Personal Values and Principles

 **WHY**

Our personal values and principles are at the centre of our work. They guide the way in which we lead our schools and work with our colleagues, pupils, parents, and wider community. The role of headteacher is often described to us as being both the best job in the world, but also sometimes the hardest. No two days are the same and the notion of being able to achieve all that we plan to in a day, or a week, is something that we must accept is rarely going to happen. Pupils only go through our classes and our school once and we must do everything we can, as school leaders, to make it the best experience that it can possibly be for every pupil in our schools. Academic outcomes are important, but the wider holistic view, preparing pupils for a rapidly changing world with the skills they will need, is also our responsibility. Our personal values and principles make us what we are, they underpin our professional life.

 # HOW

Values

In our work with headteachers we have frequently referenced the work of Stephen R. Covey, described in his book, "The seven habits of highly effective people". Although not written specifically for use in the education sector, many of his lessons are easily translated into best educational practice. His habits two and three, 'begin with the end in mind' and 'put first things first' resonate with the essential leadership focus on having clear values and principles that underpin the work of the headteacher and senior leaders and which translate into a meaningful vision for the school.

We created a diagram to demonstrate our belief that values sit at the very centre of our work as headteachers. Values underpin our vision, and our vision guides our strategic focus – our next steps, our plans for improvement which are implemented through our regular focus on priorities and future direction. The culture of the school is defined by our values – "the way we do things here".

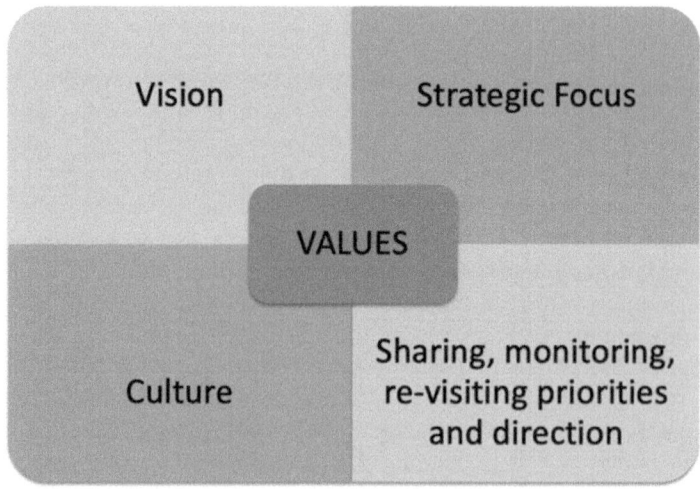

The working definitions of vision and values that we use with headteachers, and senior leaders are:

Values: What is of vital importance to your school community and team, the things you would 'go to the wall' for, for example, equality and caring.

Vision: Where we would like our school or team to be in the future; our goal or destination.

Values are not just preferences. As adults we have already formed most of the values we will ever have. We formed our values almost subconsciously and most pupils will have formed their personal values by the time they enter school.

Schools frequently list their values on their websites or display them prominently within the school. In our experience, many schools list very similar values, such as respect and care for others, showing loyalty, trust, and confidence, being fair, and working cooperatively. The work that we do with headteachers often includes unpicking these to ensure that they reflect the reality and culture within the school and are not just words. In our privileged position of being able to go into many schools, we have, on occasion, seen a very clear mismatch between the stated values and the experienced reality for some children.

Values and Visions cycle

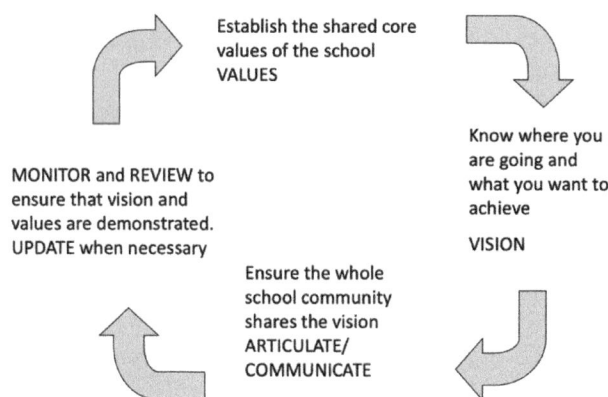

Establish the shared core values of the school
VALUES

Know where you are going and what you want to achieve

VISION

MONITOR and REVIEW to ensure that vision and values are demonstrated. UPDATE when necessary

Ensure the whole school community shares the vision
ARTICULATE/ COMMUNICATE

A values and vision cycle to support professional development, (resource bank reference 25).

One exercise that we do with headteachers is to ask them to capture a stated value of the school and then to consider what this means in everyday life and the reality of how this is shown to and by pupils, staff, and the school community.   For example, if we value equality for all, what does that mean in our school context?   How is this demonstrated to pupils – are they all able to access extracurricular activities?   Does equality for staff mean that everyone has access to effective   professional   development?   How   does   our   school demonstrate   and   celebrate   our   belief   in   equality   to   the   school community?

The values in our school:

We value	Which means	How can we evidence this value?		
		To children?	To staff?	To the school community?

A proforma to help staff unpick the stated values of the school
(Resource bank reference 26)

Vision

Many years ago, at headship interviews, a standard question was 'Describe your vision for this school.'   This always seemed an impossible question to answer – as an external headship candidate, with very little time having been spent in the school, it would seem to require huge arrogance to suggest a vision for a school, as yet, unknown.

The point of a vision is that it needs to be collective and shared by the community.   If it is simply the musings of the headteacher or senior leaders, it is not a vision.   Unless goals are clearly articulated, discussed, and understood within the school community, they cannot be achieved.   This relates to the change theory in building block nine. Unless there is a compelling reason for a change, it is unlikely to succeed.

Both vision and values are dependent upon the school culture. This is a huge area for headteachers with their senior leaders to work on, and building block six has a focus upon this.

Leadership styles

A leader is only successful if people are prepared to follow. A definition of leadership that we use is the analogy of finding a route through a dense forest. The leader creates the path through the forest; the manager follows the path that the leader has created, and the administrator tidies the path. As headteachers, we must take on all three of these roles at different times. We must define the path in our strategic leadership – decisions must be made. We must follow paths set by others, such as the Department for Education, Ofsted, the Local Authority or Trust. We also must do some path tidying – routine maintenance tasks that cannot be delegated to others. Effective leaders need a toolkit of skills and attributes that they can access as needed to support them in their role. This toolkit is informed by the leadership styles of the individual headteacher. Every leader has a range of styles, some of which relate to their innate way of leading and others which might take them out of their personal comfort zone.

There are many leadership styles identified in literature and on websites. The six that we focus upon are the ones that we were introduced to whilst working at the National College for School Leadership. These six styles were identified by Daniel Goleman, Richard Boyatzis and Annie McKee in their 2002 book "Primal Leadership". The six styles identified are visionary, coaching, affiliative, democratic, pacesetting and directive (commanding). Each of the styles has a different effect on people's emotions and each has strengths and weaknesses in different situations.

The strength of the model is in making headteachers and senior leaders aware that they need more than one leadership style. Leadership is complex and different situations require a different style of leadership. Although there are some styles that are the most 'comfortable' for an individual, it is important that leaders understand a range of styles so that they can consciously use the most effective style to resolve a specific situation.

Leadership Style	Directive	Visionary	Affiliative
Primary objective	Immediate compliance	Providing long term direction and vision	Creating harmony among leaders and staff
In a phrase:	Do what I tell you	I know where I'm going, follow me	People first, task second
Style characteristics	Lots of directions, tight control, close monitoring, top-down decision making	Leader motivates, defines standards, gives performance feedback. Leader has enthusiasm and clear vision. Sees selling the vision as key part of HT job	Sharing ideas, inspiring, trust
How it feels for staff	Little input possible, motivates by stating negative consequences of non-compliance. No creativity possible.	Highly motivating, attention focused on goals, staff aware of how their work fits into the larger vision. Leader solicits staff perspective on the vision.	Good communication: freedom to do job in own way; lots of positive feedback and praise. Poor performance can go uncorrected; mediocrity tolerated
When used ineffectively	Leader can be a bully	Can ignore skills and talents of other members of staff; leader can appear pompous and out of touch	Can lead to low standards, an appearance of favouritism, a lack of clarity and a cause of frustration
Effective when	Used in crisis situations, e.g. when informing staff what to do over the death of a teacher.	Tasks and systems in place, where new direction needed, where leader perceived to be the expert	Used as part of repertoire of styles; when giving personal help, when creating harmony among conflicting groups
Least effective when	Applied to long term tasks or with self motivated staff	Leader lacks credibility	Poor performance needs challenging; in an emergency when control is needed; when staff are task centred

Leadership Style	Democratic	Coaching	Pacesetting
Primary objective	Building a commitment among staff and generating new ideas	Long term professional development of staff	Accomplishing tasks to high standards of excellence
In a phrase:	You have the knowledge, you do it	I'll help you to do it	Task first, people second
Style characteristics	Leads by listening; high trust, respect and commitment; people buy-in	Lots of feedback and instruction; high level of delegation; staff aware of strengths and weaknesses	High performance standards; limited delegation; leader wants things done better and faster
How it feels for staff	Staff have a say in decisions; lots of flexibility and responsibility; high morale; lots of meetings; decisions by consensus; rare negative feedback	Personal long term development goals encouraged; long term learning of staff is prime motive	Poor performers identified and mot tolerated; HT expects staff to know what to do, limited feedback given
When used ineffectively	Can produce confusion, delays and conflict to lack of direction; can lead to endless meetings with little outcome, can feel leaderless	Staff unsure of what is required, standards can fall; tasks get put off	Can create extreme stress e.g. if changes needed and no discussion allowed
Effective when	Staff are competent; when they need to be well co-ordinated, when leader is uncertain about best direction and needs ideas from team	Staff are aware of areas for development and want to improve	Staff are highly motivated, competent and need little direction. Best when quick results required
Least effective when	In a crisis when immediate decisions needed; when staff need close supervision	When staff are resistant to learning or changing; when leader lacks expertise, or in a crisis when short term coercive style needed	Staff need direction and development

The six leadership styles and how to use them as a senior leader
Resource bank reference 27

One interesting issue with the leadership styles is that whilst as a leader, you may be absolutely convinced that you are demonstrating certain styles, the perception of others may be different. You may believe yourself to be primarily affiliative, but the experience of others may be that you are far more directive. There are many commercial audits available to analyse your style. The best ones are the 360-degree audits that take the opinions of other people into account when analysing your styles. Many years ago, as headteachers, we were both invited to complete a programme devised by Hay McBer, entitled "The Leadership Programme for Serving Headteachers", (LPSH). Specific members of our staff were invited to comment on our leadership including experienced and new members of staff, together with a governor, a deputy, and various others.

All had to complete a lengthy questionnaire and we had to do a similar one. The data was analysed, and over a period of several days we were given feedback on our specific leadership behaviours and competencies. Whilst this programme is no longer running, other 360-degree audits are available and can give a great deal of insight into your leadership which can help personal professional development.

For those who wish to complete a personal audit, within the online resource bank we have a leadership style inventory that will provide an initial indication of preferred styles – this may help leaders identify other styles that they may choose to develop.

Leadership Style Inventory

Score yourself on each of the following statements:

5 – I do this a lot
4 – I do this quite often
3 – I am like this sometimes
2 – This rarely describes me
1 – I am not like this at all

For each statement enter your number in the shaded box only

	Dir	Vis	Affil	Dem	Coach	Pace
I am really good at giving directions in a crisis or an emergency						
I really value peoples' feelings and take great care to look after them and praise them.						
I help staff identify their strengths and weaknesses and help them to move on in their careers.						
I motivate people by explaining how their work fits into a larger vision.						
I spend time with people to build trust and respect and to secure their commitment to our ideas.						
I set extremely high-performance standards by my example, and expect these of others.						
I am good at giving clear instructions, so people know what to do						

An extract from the leadership questionnaire
Resource bank reference 28

Emotional intelligence

Daniel Goleman's work on leadership styles built on his extensive research into emotional intelligence. He defines emotional intelligence as *"the ability to identify, assess and control one's emotions, the emotion of others and that of groups."*

Emotional intelligence is one of the vital leadership qualities that successful headteachers deploy to maximise their effectiveness. It underpins the culture of the school.

In short, it is:

"The ability to understand, accept and reorganise our own emotions and feelings, including their impact on ourselves and other people and use this knowledge to improve our own behaviours as well as to manage and improve our relationship with others".
Cartwright and Solloway, 2007

In his book, "The desert island challenge", Jeremy Sutcliffe identifies emotional intelligence as one of the eight qualities that successful school leaders exhibit.

"Successful school leaders are team builders. They understand the importance of relationships, empower those around them and show great empathy."

You cannot fulfil your role as a headteacher if you don't take your team with you. You are not capable of changing the behaviour of a single person in your team.

You can, however, adapt your own behaviour, and in response to this, your team members may choose to change their own response.

Goleman identified four key personal and interpersonal components involved in emotional intelligence – self-awareness, self-regulation, motivation, empathy, and social skills. These areas all relate to our ability to communicate and successfully manage our teams in school.

	Self	Social
Recognition	**Self-awareness** • Self-confidence • Awareness of own emotional state – accurate self-assessment • Recognising how own behaviour impacts on other people. • Being aware of how other people influence your own emotional state.	**Social awareness** • Picking up on the mood of the room/meeting • Caring about other people and their emotional situation – empathy. • Active listening – hearing what the other person is really saying.
Regulation	**Self-management** • Self-control • Flexibility • Keeping emotions in check. • Acting in line with values • Drive to succeed. • Using initiative	**Relationship management** • Handling conflict effectively. • Clearly expressing ideas/information • Being sensitive to another person's feelings (empathy) • Building bonds • Teamwork and collaboration

Four elements of emotional intelligence
Resource bank reference 29

When we work with headteachers, we always recommend that they take the time to read some of the literature around emotional intelligence. Without self-awareness – the ability to understand our own strengths, weaknesses, motivations, values, and emotions, then we cannot effectively manage our emotions – our self-management or self-regulation.   If we understand our own emotional triggers, we are more able to respond effectively to difficult situations.

Challenging conversations are an inevitable part of being a headteacher in a school. For example, if when dealing with a difficult parent or colleague, a headteacher is not able to manage their own emotions, resulting in a very heated conversation, the outcome of the meeting is unlikely to be successful. The ability to stay focused and confident, even when feeling anxious is an important leadership skill that can be developed.

Within our online resource bank, we have included an audit to support headteachers and senior leaders in beginning to self-assess aspects of their own emotional intelligence. We have taken the areas of self-awareness; self-management; social awareness and relationship management alongside the core skill of communication. When we use this with headteachers during training sessions, it always triggers powerful discussions and individual reflection.

3. Self-management

• I understand and use self-coaching techniques	[ ]
• I understand and use the differences between self-esteem and self-respect	[ ]
• I am able to become an effective role model	[ ]
• I can manage personal change effectively	[ ]
• I set personal goals and take actions towards them	[ ]
• I practise positive thinking	[ ]
• I can work effectively with my intuition	[ ]
Total (max. 35)	

An extract from our emotional intelligence audit
Resource bank reference 30

REFLECTIONS

∞ Clarity around your personal values and principles is important. It links to emotional intelligence (above) as knowing your values and principles is part of your self-awareness which is needed to manage your emotions and professional relationships.

∞ A shared vision drives school improvement – it gives direction, without this improvement can be rather ad hoc.

∞ All headteachers need an understanding of a range of leadership styles and when these are best used. Having this knowledge in your leadership toolkit makes you more effective in your work.

∞ Emotional intelligence is essential for anyone who spends their career working with others and whose impact relies upon strong professional relationships.

RESOURCES

Resource 25
A values and vision cycle to support professional development.

Resource 26
Proforma to help staff unpick the stated values of the school.

Resource 27
Leadership styles handout setting out the 6 styles.

Resource 28
Leadership style inventory.

Resource 29
Diagram to explain four of the elements of emotional intelligence.

Resource 30
Emotional intelligence audit.

 **FURTHER READING**

Stephen R. Covey, "The seven habits of highly effective people: Revised and updated 30th anniversary edition" 2020.

Daniel Goleman, "Emotional Intelligence: 25th anniversary edition", Bloomsbury publishing, 2020

Jeremy Sutcliffe, "The desert island challenge – 8 qualities of successful school leaders" Bloomsbury Education, 2013

To access **all the resources** in the **online resource bank** for a small one-off subscription just:

- ∞ email <u>headshipmatters@proton.me</u> or
- ∞ visit www.tinyurl.com/3vtzknpu or
- ∞ scan the QR code below

Teaching and Learning Matters

**WHY**

The Education Inspection Framework (2019) firmly put the emphasis of the judgement of the effectiveness of schools on the quality of the education provided for pupils. Leadership and management are largely measured by how well headteachers and senior leaders ensure that this is the absolute priority and, as importantly, how they know about the quality of education in their schools. This can only be informed by highly effective and efficient monitoring.

 **HOW**

We have developed a time-saving resource, "The teaching over time evaluation matrix" or, TOTEM for short, that enables leaders to record all aspects of their monitoring of provision in a transparent, systematic, and consistent way. It is also personalised to the needs of the individual teacher allowing for strengths and areas of development to be recorded and tracked, providing the next steps for improvement, which can also be used to support the performance management process.

We have created five dimensions, each of which has a series of elements to be monitored. Each element has several statements against which descriptors at four different levels from ineffective through to highly effective are provided. These link closely to the Ofsted quality judgements. Each statement is also linked to the National Teacher Standards.

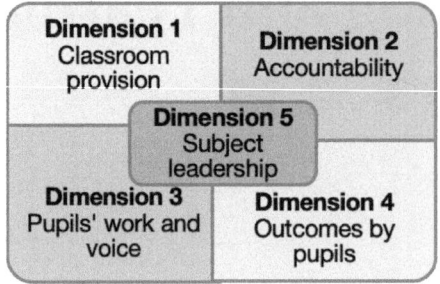

Monitoring is always about applying professional judgement, and the descriptors within the effectiveness spectrum ensure that whoever is carrying out the monitoring, is doing so consistently which in turn gives those being monitored confidence in the system. This resource is frequently used by teachers to self-evaluate their effectiveness in the five dimensions as it provides them with clear indicators of how to become more effective within that dimension. There are further explanatory notes available, (resource bank reference 31).

As headteachers, we all recognise that any teacher can have a bad day or deliver an occasional weak lesson. This does not make them an ineffective teacher. The point of TOTEM is that it records multiple lesson visits over the period of a term or an academic year enabling all teachers to demonstrate their effectiveness.

The total flexibility of the system also means that it is perfectly acceptable to carry out monitoring exercises more often with some teachers than others in relation to their individual development needs.

This ensures that the person carrying out the monitoring uses their monitoring time as effectively as possible.

Examples, (extracts only), of four of the five dimensions are detailed below to provide an insight to the comprehensive resource. This comprehensive and intuitive resource is available from our resource bank, (resource bank reference 33). Also, within the resource bank there is a short PowerPoint presentation to support headteachers when introducing the TOTEM resource, (resource bank reference 32).

Dimension 1: Classroom provision – quality, expectations, consistency.
(Evidence gathered through lesson visits; learning walks; environment checks and other systems of direct observation)

Ref	Question / Aspect	Ineffective	Partially Effective	Effective	Highly Effective
1.1	How well demonstrated is the teacher's subject knowledge and is this well communicated to pupils? How does the teacher link prior knowledge to new learning, enabling the lesson to be correctly pitched? Does the teacher use retrieval strategies? TS3	Subject knowledge is insecure and there are significant gaps in knowledge delivery with pupils. Communication is sometimes weak. Little evidence of awareness of pupil's prior knowledge and lesson pitch is inaccurate.	Teacher has insufficient subject knowledge to teach subjects well. Teacher has not got sufficient awareness of pupil's prior knowledge resulting in the lesson offering little learning challenge or support to pupils.	Secure subject knowledge is used to sustain pupils' interest and challenge thinking and is well communicated to pupils. Evidence of good understanding of prior knowledge and pitch of lesson accurate.	Deep knowledge and subject expertise is demonstrated and communicated well to pupils to provide excellent learning opportunities. Teacher fully aware of prior knowledge and pitch of lesson meets needs of all pupils.
1.2	Are expectations of pupils suitably high, and consistent, evidenced through clear, concise learning objectives? Is the lesson delivered in small chunks enabling pupils to grasp new learning in a logical sequence of steps? TS1	Expectations are too low and pupils underperform as a consequence. Sequencing of learning not evident. Learning objectives unclear.	Inconsistent expectations of pupils and content of lesson not sufficiently demanding. Lack of clarity in learning objectives.	Generally high expectations of what all pupils can achieve resulting in pupils learning well with lesson content offering logical sequence and challenge to pupils. Clear concise learning objectives impact on learning.	Consistently high expectations and demanding content, logically sequenced ensures that all pupils achieve, irrespective of ability. Lessons inspire, motivate and challenge all pupils. Learning objectives clear and concise matching lesson content.
1.3	How effectively are pupils learning? Is there tangible evidence of learning i.e. knowing more and remembering more and is the focus of the lesson clearly understood by pupils? TS1	Very few pupils appear to be learning as the lesson and tasks are not matched to learning needs.	Significant proportion of pupils unable to demonstrate learning through the lesson; this may be due to a mismatch between the task and learning needs.	Tangible evidence of pupils learning because tasks are matched well to learning needs.	All pupils are challenged because learning needs are met exceptionally well. This results in tangible evidence of learning in all pupil groups.
1.4	Does on-going formative assessment (e.g. 'live' or 'in the moment' feedback) provide opportunities that enable the teacher to check	Little or no examples of formative assessment either verbal or written to individuals or groups resulting in unclear next steps for learning.	Assessment is inconsistent and does not help to identify what pupils need to learn next.	Formative assessment by adults and pupils enables learning to progress at a suitable pace. It is differentiated by ability and	Assessment is on-going, timely and highly effective in moving pupils' learning on at a rapid and sustained pace.

Dimension 2: Accountability processes – principles, expectations, impact
(evidence gathered through pupil progress meeting discussions and other discussions around the quality of teaching and learning)

Ref	Question / Aspect	Ineffective	Partially Effective	Effective	Highly Effective
2.1	How accurate are the teacher's assessments? Do they enable teachers to produce clear next steps for pupils? Do they help pupils embed knowledge and use it in subsequent tasks? TS6	Purpose of assessment unclear as it does not inform next steps for pupils. Assessments are not in line with school moderation and have minimal impact on future learning.	Some evidence that a small number of pupils' needs are being accurately assessed but this is not consistent and sometimes results in next steps planning being inaccurate.	Assessed with accuracy but not always fully or consistently resulting in missed opportunities in planning next steps in learning. Assessment generally has a positive impact on planning for next steps in learning.	Consistently with a high degree of accuracy, endorsed through moderation and test data. This results in accurate next steps planning and impacts upon learning. Pupils understand assessments and can talk about impact on learning.
2.2	How well presented are cases for proposed action e.g. interventions? TS5	Poor presentation based on insufficient knowledge of individual needs and pupils' context and current achievements.	Presentation is incomplete and lacks coherence regarding the most appropriate action.	Cases for intervention made but sometimes lack sufficient detail.	Coherent and well-constructed proposals that focus on intended outcomes in response to additional interventions.
2.3	How effective is the teacher at implementing intervention processes? Does the teacher ensure that interventions do not narrow the curriculum for pupils? TS5	Weak implementation with little or no impact on improving pupil outcomes. Pupils often taken out from the same lessons consequently narrowing their curriculum.	Teacher is able to implement interventions with close supervision from a line manager. Teacher needs to be more aware of what children might miss when removed from class for interventions.	Consistent in ensuring interventions match needs and have a positive impact. Interventions usually in the classroom ensuring children access the full curriculum.	Strong track record of implementing actions and deploying additional adults both in and out of the classroom. Monitoring effective with positive results achieved as intended.
2.4	How well does the teacher use additional adults to deliver intervention strategies? Is consideration given to when and where interventions take place? TS8	Poor co-ordination and communication results in haphazard use of additional adults and intervention strategies, resulting in lack of impact upon achievement outcomes.	Additional adults seek constant direction from the teacher. Little evidence of forward thinking and sharing of planning. Interventions have little impact on outcomes	Additional adults are used effectively and provide intervention support programmes in a confident well-informed manner that meets pupils' needs.	Highly effective communication of expectations and ways of working results in pupils responding well to strategies to improve outcomes. Additional adults feel valued.

53

Dimension 3: Pupils' work and voice – quality, expectations, consistency

(evidence gathered mostly through book scrutiny and discussions with pupils)

	Question / Aspect	Ineffective	Partially Effective	Effective	Highly Effective
3.1	Is there an adequate range of differentiation by design/ability range/individual need? Are teachers skilled enough so that they can adapt their teaching to meet the range of needs without unnecessarily individualised approaches? TS5	Work scrutiny shows little or no differentiation. Learning is predominantly evidenced by outcome. Pupil's understanding is not checked sufficiently resulting in limited learning and time wasted.	Attempts made to differentiate by task but this is ineffective in terms of supporting learners at different levels. Poor planning and curriculum design indicates lack of ambition for some pupils.	Mostly differentiated by task over time resulting in clear progress in lessons for all ability groups with coherent planning leading to development of long-term memory.	Differentiation by task is highly effective and embedded across the whole subject over time. Differing abilities are well catered for, reflected from coherent, well structured planning to workbook contents.
3.2	How comprehensively is the school curriculum being covered? Is it sufficiently ambitious and designed to support pupils in acquiring skills, knowledge and understanding in all subjects? TS3	Inconsistent attention to subject coverage with little or no coherence over time. Books do not demonstrate appropriate coverage and lessons are unconnected with no apparent sequencing of learning.	Partial evidence of curriculum coverage in some subjects but inconsistent across the whole school curriculum.	Coverage is effective in most areas but gaps exist in some subjects.	Thorough planning resulting in carefully constructed learning based on prior knowledge is evident in all workbooks over time. Curriculum coverage is complete.
3.3	Is there clear evidence of sequencing and systematic progression within each subject? TS3	Systematic progression not evident – content of books appears a random series of tasks	Evidence of some progression and sequencing but insufficient to secure high quality learning.	Evidence of planned progression and sequencing of work but not always consistent across subjects.	Curriculum sequencing and systematic progression evident in all subjects leading to high quality learning.
3.4	To what extent is there a suitable range and variety of learning activities that embed the cultural capital specified by the school? TS4	Little or no evidence of a range of learning activities. Singular approach dominates the teaching style, often worksheets or over dependence upon published schemes.	Some variation in learning opportunities but not a full repertoire employed. Limited opportunities identified to build cultural capital.	Learning activities are often varied but not consistent within or across subjects. Cultural capital being addressed through the curriculum.	Learning activities are richly varied over time, embedding cultural capital and matching ability needs and subject requirements.
3.5	Is marking in-line with school policy? TS6	Little or no compliance with policy, little or no marking other than ticks and 'well	Marking sometimes follows policy but is inconsistent.	Marking follows school policy but is not always consistent across the class.	High quality marking with constructive feedback which

Dimension 4: Outcomes by pupils – gaps, in line with, better than/below ARE + national, progress

(evidence gathered through on-going data analysis, both summative and formative)

Ref	Question / Aspect	Ineffective	Partially Effective	Effective	Highly Effective
4.1	Are pupils attaining inline with age related expectations? TS6	Gaps are not being narrowed or closed, resulting in very few pupils attaining in line with age related and school expectations.	Some pupils are achieving in-line with age related expectations but few strategies being seen to increase the proportion over the year.	Most pupils are achieving in-line with age and school related expectations for both attainment and progress.	Data shows gaps are rapidly narrowing and/or closing as a result of consistently better than good teaching. Almost all pupils are achieving in-line with expectations.
4.2	How well are the most able/disadvantaged pupils being catered for? TS5	Little or no ability based differentiation resulting a growing gap between peers and national benchmarks. Little or no evidence of ability matched learning.	Minimal differentiated provision resulting in able pupils plateauing and failing to advance rapidly and disadvantaged not achieving all of which they are capable.	Support and challenge effectively provided. Most able pupils attain well and show progress, which matches their ability levels, disadvantaged pupils access a full curriculum resulting in expected progress.	Differentiated practice accurately matched to needs of different abilities. Pupils provided with carefully constructed learning opportunities and challenges that enable them to achieve at and above expectations.
4.3	To what extent are pupils showing consistent and adequate rates of progress over time in all core subjects, from recognised starting points TS2	Little or no progress seen through assessment data over time, resulting in pupils either "standing still" or regressing.	Inconsistent rates of progress result in a significant number of pupils attaining below expectations. Some evidence of pupils responding well but not in a uniform manner.	The vast majority of pupils progress in-line with age related and school expectations from accepted prior attainment starting points.	Irrespective of ability, pupils progress consistently well in response to better than good quality teaching over time.
4.4	Are pupils making sufficient and sustained progress throughout the year in foundation subjects? How well is achievement in foundation subjects being assessed? TS6	Insufficient progress across ability bands; little or no assessment resulting in inaccurate information being generated resulting in incomplete pupil profile.	Inconsistent progress across subjects. Some assessment undertaken but not in all foundation subjects and evidence of some inaccuracies in assessment.	Most pupils show good progress over time from starting points. Assessments are undertaken and are largely accurate across most subjects.	The vast majority of pupils achieve in-line with or above expectations across all foundation subjects. School's data collection system used effectively.

Dimension 1
Classroom provision – quality, expectations, consistency.

Dimension 2
Accountability processes – principles, expectations, impact.

Dimension 3
Pupils' work and voice – quality, expectations, consistency

Dimension 4
Outcomes by pupils – gaps, in line with, better than/below ARE + national, progress.

Dimension 5
Subject leadership – this dimension is explored in detail throughout building block three.

There is also an Early Years Foundation Stage, (EYFS), set of descriptors, created by EYFS practitioners, to make the resource relevant to that phase, (resource bank reference 34).

Headteachers who are using this resource already, are doing so in different ways. The resource is sufficiently flexible for headteachers to pick and choose the elements that are most important in their own context. Some choose to install the dimensions onto their iPad or laptop, (as it is an Excel spreadsheet), and use it to record electronically whilst in the classroom, (if monitoring dimension 1). They would highlight the most appropriate descriptor statement that best fits the evidence being gathered.

Alternatively, some headteachers take a printed copy of dimension 1 into the classroom with them and physically highlight the most appropriate descriptors, based on the evidence gathered, and then use that subsequently to draft a lesson visit report.

Used in any way, this resource will enable a picture of the quality of teaching over time to be established that charts the progress made by each teacher.

Since introducing this resource, we know that some headteachers have found it of immense value in carrying out one of the most challenging tasks of school leaders – creating an evidence bank that may be needed if a teacher is going through a capability process. It enables the school to show how they are supporting the teacher and, sadly, when a teacher simply can't perform at the required standard despite this support.

As part of this resource, we have also created a teacher development record that enables key points for development to be recorded and acted upon. This then becomes the property of the teacher to maintain and share, possibly as part of an appraisal or performance management process. Sample extract below, (resource bank reference 35).

Dimension 2: Accountability processes – principles, expectations, impact
(evidence largely gathered through pupil progress meeting discussions and other discussions around quality of teaching and learning)

Question / Aspect	Notable evidence with dates	RAGB AUT	RAGB SPR	RAGB SUM	Actions for improvement by...
2.1 How accurate are the teacher's assessments? Do they enable teachers to produce clear next steps for pupils? Do they help pupils embed knowledge and use it in subsequent tasks? TS6	Oct 19 Generally accurate but not always an explicit link to next steps Dec 19 Improving links evident in workbooks Feb 20 Evidence in books to show impact of assessments; repeated June 20	A	G	G	Ensure link between assessment and next steps is made – revisit Dec 10 Final book scrutiny to check links June 20
2.2 How well presented are cases for proposed action? E.g. interventions? TS5	Consistently effective	G	G	G	
2.3 How effective is the teacher at implementing intervention processes? Does the teacher ensure that interventions do not narrow the curriculum for pupils? TS5	Nov 19 Concern that same group of children consistently working on intervention during music lessons Jan 20 Timetables reorganised, more interventions in classroom	A	G	G	Monitor to ensure curriculum not narrowed for identified pupils. Jan 20
2.4 How well does the teacher use additional adults to deliver intervention strategies? Is consideration given to when and where interventions take place? TS8	Dec 19 Additional adults used effectively, clear of expectations of teacher	G	G	G	
2.5 Are parents provided with clear and timely information on how well their child is progressing? TS8	Consistently effective	G	G	G	
2.6 How well are disadvantaged pupils being catered for? Is the curriculum sufficiently ambitious for disadvantaged pupils, including those with SEND? TS5	Consistently effective	G	G	G	
2.7 To what extent is prior achievement	Oct 19 Prior achievement not always				Monitor to ensure priori achievement

Provision of feedback
Ways to structure developmental feedback conversations

One of the clear outcomes of undertaking the monitoring of teaching over time is not only to judge the quality of provision, but also to generate feedback for teachers with the intention of improving the quality of their practice. Feedback is a gift. Teachers can choose to accept it and work on their points for improvement, or not accept it, as the case may be. By providing the developmental feedback, headteachers and senior leaders have a legitimate line of enquiry when they next visit the teacher's classroom.

Scaffold one

CSS or 'continue, stop and start…' This model is one where the leader is dominating the conversation and is being instructional rather than being a coach. This scaffold is most frequently used with teachers in the early stages of their career where they are still learning their craft of teaching. Where appropriate, provide specific examples of what is effective and therefore to be continued. Provide examples of evidence potentially contrary to school policy, or actions that are hindering pupils' learning, and therefore to be stopped. Provide positive suggestions/expectations of new behaviour, (possibly referencing exemplary evidence from other staff), and specify a time for a repeated scrutiny to check on all three aspects.

Scaffold two

WWW/EBI or "what is working well / even better if…" This model is a more engaging conversation with a distinct coaching approach. The observer asks for examples of effective practice from the teacher and either agrees or shares other examples that he/she noticed. A similar approach is to ask the teacher what he/she would improve/change if the lesson was to be repeated. Again, the observer agrees or provides examples of more effective practice.

Scaffold three

CBI or "context, behaviour, impact". This is the process of citing a worked example as seen in a pupil's book that you want to see more of in all pupils' books. The context is the planned learning activity, evidenced by the learning objective, planned outcome etc. Behaviour is what the teacher did during the lesson, (as recorded in the plan and in individual pupils' work), and the impact is what the teacher intervention, (behaviour), resulted in. An example of this might be:
The **context** is the teaching of a simple grammatical rule. A middle ability pupil was tasked to write a sentence for each word to show they understood the correct use. The teacher intervened, **(behaviour),** after the pupil had written two sentences, as s/he had noticed the pupil was not applying appropriate learning. This intervention was evidenced through written comments from the teacher to confirm the discussion with the pupil. The **impact** of this action was that the pupil completed the remaining six sentences in line with the intended outcomes.

The feedback 'sandwich'

Sometimes, when giving feedback to colleagues, there are some hard messages to relay. Teachers are often the harshest critics of their own performance but there are still occasions when giving honest feedback is difficult. One technique that we have used is the well-known feedback sandwich. For example, following a relatively poor lesson visit, you start with a positive from the lesson visit recognising a good aspect of practice seen. You then address the areas that need to be improved and finally you end with some ideas and suggestions to help improve the weak area. The important point if using this technique is to be clear. The teacher must walk away with absolute clarity on what needs to be improved. This technique is not right for every situation – for example if there are multiple areas of concern,

REFLECTIONS

∞ It is essential to monitor the quality of teaching over time.
∞ The use of a clearly defined spectrum of effectiveness helps arrive at quality judgements quickly.
∞ Self-evaluation by teachers using the matrix enable reflection and recognition of their next steps.
∞ Feedback must be provided and be developmental with a drive to change and improve practice.

RESOURCES

Resource 31
Teaching over Time Evaluation Matrix (TOTEM) explanatory notes.

Resource 32
A PowerPoint presentation about TOTEM.

Resource 33
Descriptor statements for the five dimensions of TOTEM.
 ∞ Classroom provision
 ∞ Accountability processes
 ∞ Pupils' work and pupil voice
 ∞ Pupil outcomes
 ∞ Quality of subject leadership

Resource 34
Descriptor statements for the Early Years Foundation Stage.

Resource 35
Sample of a teacher development record for dimension 1.

To access **all the resources** in the **online resource bank** for a small one-off subscription just:

- ∞ email <u>headshipmatters@proton.me</u> or
- ∞ visit www.tinyurl.com/3vtzknpu or
- ∞ scan the QR code below

Building Block **3**

Subject Leadership Matters

**WHY**

Expectations and principles

The role of the subject leader in primary schools, together with the expectations of the role have changed enormously over the span of our careers. Subject leadership is now an intrinsic part of the role of the classroom teacher and there is an expectation that all teachers, other than those newest to the profession, take on this role.

This is not for Ofsted – it's about your teachers being the best subject leaders they can be so that the children get the best possible teaching. However, we are accountable to Ofsted and within the 'good' judgement for quality of education, the judgement is that *"teachers have good knowledge of the subject(s) and courses they teach."* This is further re-iterated in the current (2012) Teacher Standards:

"Teachers make the education of their pupils their first concern and are accountable for achieving the highest possible standards in work and conduct. Teachers act with honesty and integrity; have strong subject knowledge, keep their knowledge and skills as teachers up-to-date and are self-critical; forge positive professional relationships; and work with parents in the best interests of their pupils."

The key change in the importance of the role emerged from the changing expectations of the education inspection framework. Whereas a few years ago, most conversations with inspectors involved the headteacher and senior team, the expectation now is that all subject leaders can articulate, with confidence, information about their subject, e.g. curriculum design, effectiveness of the implementation of the curriculum and the impact of the school curriculum, in readiness for a deep dive inspection. They are also invited to take an active part in the inspection by accompanying inspectors into classrooms.

This change has resulted in the expectation that senior leaders proactively develop subject leaders so that they can support the inspection process.

For the last few iterations of the School Inspection Handbook within the 'good' judgement for leadership and management, the requirement is that:

"Leaders focus on improving teachers' subject, pedagogical and pedagogical content knowledge to enhance the teaching of the curriculum and the appropriate use of assessment. The practice and subject knowledge of staff, including ECTs, build and improve over time."

Our interpretation of this is that subject leaders must firstly have access to professional development opportunities to develop their personal subject knowledge so that they can effectively lead their subjects. Secondly, all teachers need to receive professional development to give them a good understanding of pedagogy – the method and practice of teaching, for example, teaching approaches, knowledge of teaching theory and feedback and assessment. Thirdly, teachers need support in developing pedagogical content knowledge – the way teachers relate their pedagogical knowledge to their subject matter knowledge i.e. there is a different in approach to teaching PE compared with mathematics.

We were asked by a colleague to set out our expectations of a subject leader, we responded as follows:

The first thing we would want you to do is to set out the intent, implementation, and impact for your subject. The current Education Inspection Framework is centred around these three areas within the quality of education judgement. Some schools have written whole school statements incorporating these three 'I's. One purpose of this is to get subject leaders to think deeply about their subject, why they teach it in the way that they do and why this is right for the context of the individual school.

The Intent is about what you, as a school, want for your children, in your subject by certain points e.g. end of year, end of key stage.
'The knowledge and skills that pupils will gain at each stage through the school's curriculum' (School Inspection Handbook, January 2024, paragraph 235).

The Implementation is how you do it - how do you arrange teaching? How is your curriculum planned, for example, whether or not you use commercial schemes and if so, why have you chosen the ones that you have? Are children put in ability sets for some subjects? Do you have cross curricular themes etc?

'How the curriculum developed or adopted by the school is taught and assessed in order to support pupils to build their knowledge and apply that knowledge as skills.' (SIH Jan 2024 paragraph 236)

Impact is the 'so what' - what have you achieved because of your intent and implementation?
'The outcomes that pupils achieve as a result of the education they have received.' (SIH Jan 2024 paragraph 237)

- ∞ *We would expect you to have a file containing all of the relevant information about your subject, this is for your reference purposes and to share with colleagues as needed.*
- ∞ *We would expect you, as subject lead, to complete an annual subject audit.*

Using this -

∞ *We would expect you to create and monitor an annual subject improvement plan.*

We would expect to see evidence of your monitoring of the subject, for example, book scrutinies; lesson visits; learning walks; pupil voice etc. The amount of monitoring should be manageable – more for the core subjects and a lighter touch for the foundation subjects. We would want you to be able to articulate any tangible improvements because of your monitoring e.g. something you've become aware of that you have then changed to improve teaching and learning in the subject.

We would expect to talk to you about the support and professional development that you offer to support and develop colleagues in your subject.

We would expect that you are being proactive in keeping yourself updated with changes in your subject; for example, having accessed the latest Ofsted subject reports and being aware of any easily available subject research, such as through the Education Endowment Foundation. You may have accessed some research that you are applying – evidence informed practice is becoming increasing important.

In the foundation subjects, we would expect to see a subject progression map, showing age related expectations at the end of each year in terms of the development of skills in the different aspects of your subject. (Core subjects are different with a huge amount of detail existing within the actual national curriculum)

We might expect you to have an exemplar file demonstrating age related expectations in your subject in different year groups This is really useful to share with teachers new to the school or year group to show what age-related expectations or what greater depth look like. It doesn't need to be huge, but pieces of work should be annotated so that it is clear what is being demonstrated. A good exemplar file can show expectations, progress, and differentiation.
All the above needs to be something you can talk about with confidence.

In writing our response to the question, we referenced the set of resources we had created to support subject leaders. We often carry out 1-1 subject leader interviews in schools and our own learning from these has helped us to create this suite of materials.

 **HOW**

Training resources

Our first resource is a PowerPoint presentation (see resource bank reference 37), the aims of which are to clarify:

- The role of subject leaders and their responsibilities e.g. developing the curriculum for the subject.
- Demonstrating the leadership of the subject.
- Some key elements of subject leadership – subject planning; subject audits; improvement plans; subject files; monitoring; evidence-informed practice.

We would suggest that this could be used either across two staff meetings, or as a focus for a professional development day on subject leadership. It considers the core functions of subject leaders; unpicks why we need effective subject leaders, referencing both the School Inspection Handbook (January 2024) and the Teacher Standards. It then reflects on curriculum and planning with a focus on skills and knowledge.

The issue of accountability and the importance of a subject leader audit and the ability of the subject leader to demonstrate impact, leading to the creation of a subject improvement plan are the next areas covered. There is then reference to the inspection process and deep dives and finally the practical issues of subject leader files; evidence; essential documentation for subject leaders and how subject leaders can develop their subjects using evidence informed practice.

A subject audit proforma

This is a proforma that we ask subject leaders to complete before we meet with them to discuss their leadership. It acts as a self-evaluation tool for the subject leader and can help identify next steps. This can also feed into the performance management process. We would suggest that this is completed annually by all subject leaders.

As a subject leader, to what extent ...

	1 Strongly established	2 Developing well	3 Emerging	4 Needing improvement
Can you describe your aims and ambition for your subject (intent)				
Can you articulate the curriculum design for your subject in school? Why do you teach the subject in the way that you do? Why have you selected specific resources e.g. schemes? (implementation)				
Is there a clear sequence/logical progression of learning in your subject throughout children's time in the school? Do teachers build on prior learning?				
Do you, as subject leader, have the knowledge, expertise and skill to design and implement the subject curriculum?				

Subject leadership audit proforma
Resource bank reference 38

Subject leader questions

All subject leaders need to be able to articulate information about their subjects. They need to be able to do this to different audiences including colleagues; governors; parents and, on occasion, to inspectors. The senior leaders in the school need to give their subject leaders the opportunity to do this regularly so that confidence grows – our experience is that the first-time subject leaders are asked to talk about different aspects of their subjects, they find this difficult. The key is to develop them so that they can be concise but informative and ensure that the relevant points are described. We have created several generic sets of questions – a sample is below, and full versions are in the online resource bank, including those for early years practitioners and special educational needs coordinators.

GENERAL QUESTIONS

What will I see in a *name of subject* lesson at *name of school*?

Show me that learning intentions are clear and followed

Show me an example of how misconceptions are addressed

Can you demonstrate that actual taught and learned coverage match intended coverage, i.e. link from the progression map?

Can you show me an example of sequencing of knowledge or a skill over time?

What strategies are being used to build long-term memory in your subject?

Can you show me an example of revisiting earlier learning?

Are transitions between year groups in your subject smooth – show me

Are the expectations the same in all year groups e.g. presentation etc.

Show me some evidence of key subject vocabulary and how this is developed across year groups.

Sample of generic questions for subject leaders
Resource bank reference 39

A subject improvement plan

This is the same format as we outlined in the foundation stone for school improvement planning. The process is the same but somewhat shorter.

Our belief is that the subject improvement plan should be created following an audit of the subject and in response to what has been seen through monitoring. As with the school improvement plan, the first question is 'what is the compelling reason for this improvement?', the second question is 'what will the impact be when it is in place?' and the third, 'how are we going to get there? i.e. the steps needed to achieve successful and sustainable change.

We would suggest that there should be no more than three issues to be addressed and that to keep the process manageable, subject leaders do a brief progress update each term on the back of the proforma.

With any improvement plan, remember they are works in progress – we really like seeing crossings out and additions over time – we find these useful to demonstrate real improvement and a recognition that things can change once an issue starts to be addressed.

Subject Improvement Plan 2024-25

For Successful and Sustainable Change to take place there need to be 3 non-negotiable elements:
1. A compelling reason for the change
2. A clear vision of the future with the change in place i.e. the impact
3. A coherent Action Plan identifying the steps needed

What is the issue / context / compelling reason?	What difference are we intending to make? (Impact)	The actions we will implement to achieve the impact are...			
		What will be completed? How this will be achieved?	Who will lead on this and who will support?	When this will take place? (including milestones)	Cost – overall and at each stage

Subject improvement plan - Resource bank reference 42

PROGRESS MADE ON IDENTIFIED AREAS OF IMPROVEMENT AND IMPACT ON TEACHING AND LEARNING:

	Autumn term	Spring term	Summer term
Area 1 Progress Next Steps			
Area 2 Progress Next steps:			
Area 3 Progress Next steps:			

All comments in the boxes should relate to impact of your work in the subject. Dates need to be included wherever possible. A copy to be given to SLT at the end of every term.

Progress update for the plan - Resource bank reference 42

Contents in the subject file

When we spend time monitoring subject leadership in schools, we always ask the subject leader to bring along their file or any documentation relating to their subject. There are a variety of responses to this request. Sometimes we are presented with bulging folders of everything that has ever related to the subject over a great many years, often led by a completely different leader. The material in these folders is often outdated, rarely looked at, and serves little purpose. At other times we meet with subject leaders who ask for some guidance on what should be in the file. We created a list of documents that we feel are useful. It is not an exhaustive list and there may be items on this that your subject leaders don't need or want, but it can act as a starter for ten in terms of creating folders.

We would also recommend that a school aims for a level of consistency in the subject folders that are kept. This makes it easier for subject leaders to work together and for colleagues to find what they need in a particular folder.

Subject Leader Folder – some suggested contents and organisation

1. **Subject overview**
   - A copy of the school's current subject policy – make sure that it references why the curriculum is designed in the way that it is for the context of the school . We would suggest creating a 3 'I's statement with your intent, implementation and impact clarified (see the handout in the pack on drafting this statement)

2. **The big picture**
   - Any relevant subject part of the School Improvement Plan or reference from last Ofsted report to the subject (if there was one)

3. **Action plans, impact and review**
   - Current improvement/action plan for the subject
   - Termly reviews of progress of the plan

4. **Planning**
   - Your subject progression map, showing the logical sequencing of skills in each year group.
   - A copy of any scheme of work e.g. NC with adaptations or school specific SOW or references to any commercial schemes or knowledge organiser used to support your planning.
   - A long-term overview or curriculum map showing what topics/units will be delivered during the year and when they will be delivered
   - A sample of teacher's planning – medium term/short term

Suggested contents and organisation of a subject leaders' file
Resource bank reference 44

Descriptors of effective subject leadership

Building block two, the quality of teaching and learning, has a focus on how senior leaders make judgements during learning walks and lesson visits. We have always believed that this process must be fair, transparent, and developmental. We therefore include in our subject leader building block the grid that headteachers and senior leaders may use when making judgements of subject leadership over time.

Dimension 5: Subject Leadership

(evidence gathered through discussions with teachers; subject documentation; staff meetings; planning meetings etc.)

Ref	Question / Aspect	Ineffective	Partially Effective	Effective	Highly Effective
5.1	Can the Subject Leader (SL) articulate curriculum intent for their subject - what pupils should know, understand and be able to do at key points in time e.g. end of year, key stage etc? TS3	Not able to articulate in any meaningful way, the curriculum intent	Is starting to understand the need to be able to define subject intent but needs considerable support to do this effectively	SL is able to articulate curriculum intent and to give a clear picture of what the school is aiming to provide for pupils.	A high degree of understanding of subject intent which is clearly articulated to staff, governors and parents. This vision drives the subject.
5.2	Is the SL able to describe the curriculum design and how this has developed within the context of the school? TS3	Does not have a grasp of why and how the subject is designed or how it has developed. Can only relate curriculum design to own class/year group.	Is starting to gain an understanding of the curriculum design but cannot give the big picture across the whole school beyond identifying published schemes used.	Has a good understanding of the design and development of the curriculum and is able to support staff in further developing it.	Has a comprehensive understanding of curriculum design and development. Is the lead practitioner in further developing the curriculum - strongly related to local context and needs.
5.3	Can the SL identify both strengths and areas of development for the subject? TS3	No clear understanding of either strengths or areas of development, no evidence of planning to identify these.	Is able to identify key strengths and areas of development but without the depth necessary to then develop/resolve these.	Can clearly outline both strengths and areas of development within the subject and is taking the lead in both areas.	Has completed thorough self-evaluation to ensure that the strengths and areas of development identified are accurate and there is a live improvement plan is in place to utilise/support both.
5.4	Does the SL have a clear action plan for improvement that is implemented with measurable impact? TS3	This is not yet in place, linked to 5.3.	A basic improvement plan building on 5.3 is in place but greater awareness of subject needed to ensure it meets needs and will have impact.	An effective plan is in place, which is fit-for-purpose and allows SL to report on impact of identified improvement areas.	Highly effective improvement plan is being implemented; regular impact updates given, and plans adapted as needs change.
5.5	Is the SL able to identify the curriculum development needs of staff and how these will be addressed? TS8	SL has not identified the curriculum development needs of staff in any meaningful way.	SL has identified some curriculum development needs e.g. lack of subject knowledge amongst some members of staff but has not yet addressed these.	SL has identified key curriculum development areas for staff and has planned some CPD to address these.	Highly effective subject leadership ensure that development needs are known and range of CPD is arranged to meet these. Staff confident in SL's ability to support them in developing subject knowledge.

The first half of the teaching over time evaluation matrix, (TOTEM),
dimension 5, judging the quality of subject leadership
Resource bank reference 45

 **REFLECTIONS**

∞ Subject leadership is now an intrinsic part of the role of the classroom teacher and there is an expectation that headteachers and senior leaders support staff in developing skills and knowledge to enable them to be effective in the role.
∞ The Teacher Standards (2012) expect that subject leaders have strong subject knowledge and keep their knowledge and skills as teachers up to date.
∞ Carrying out the role of subject leader is time-consuming and resources that make this easier will reduce teacher workload.
∞ Using a set of resources such as the ones we have created, support consistency and collaboration across all subjects.

 **RESOURCES**

Resource 36
Model of the effective subject leadership cycle.

Resource 37
A PowerPoint presentation on the role of the subject leader.

Resource 38
A subject leadership audit proforma.

Resource 39
A generic set of questions for subject leaders to respond to.

Resource 40
Quality of Education EYFS questions.

Resource 41
Suggested SENDCo questions (mainstream example).

Resource 42
A blank subject improvement plan with progress update.

Resource 43
A sample subject improvement plan.

Resource 44
Our suggestions for the contents of a subject file.

Resource 45
Dimension 5, judging the quality of subject leadership over time.

Resource 46
Drafting intent, implementation impact statements.

Resource 47
A copy of the Teacher Standards overview.

 # FURTHER READING

Tom Sherrington, "Rosenshine's principles in action", John Catt publishing, 2019

Mike Bell, "The fundamentals of teaching, a five-step model", Routledge 2021

To access **all the resources** in the **online resource bank** for a small one-off subscription just:

- ∞ email headshipmatters@proton.me or
- ∞ visit www.tinyurl.com/3vtzknpu or
- ∞ scan the QR code below

Performance Management Matters

We use the terms "appraisal" and "performance management" interchangeably in this building block. The two terms refer to the same process, and, within the school context, mean the same thing.

Teacher appraisal

 **WHY**

Performance management, (appraisal), is the process of assessing the overall performance of a teacher in the context of the individual's job description and any relevant pay progression criteria and making plans for the individual's future development in the context of the school's improvement plan. National Teacher Standards provide the backdrop to discussions about performance and future development. The standards define the professional attributes, knowledge, understanding and skills for all teachers. Professional development opportunities support achieving objectives, improving teaching and furthering career progression and succession planning.

All teachers need to be able to answer the following questions:

- ∞ *"What do I need to do to improve the quality of my teaching to always be good or better?*
- ∞ *What is the quality of professional development in this school?"*

Professional development is not just about courses. See our detailed exploration of this later in this building block. It includes monitoring systems; marking trawls; peer observations; school visits and anything else that you have done to develop and improve teaching.

The National Teacher Standards apply to teachers regardless of career stage and define the minimum level of practice expected of teachers from qualified teacher status onwards.

Headteachers assess teachers against the standards in line with what should reasonably be expected of a teacher in the relevant role and at an identified stage of their career (e.g. early career teacher through to upper pay spine teachers). The professional judgement of headteachers and appraisers is central to appraisal against these standards – consistency is essential for a fair and transparent system.

 **HOW**

The performance management process should be developed to fit the context of the individual school, however, there will be some key elements this annual cycle that are common to all schools.

The first item within our resource for supporting performance management is a generic PowerPoint presentation of the key issues, which can be adapted by schools (see resource bank reference 48).

We have also provided a sample of some possible areas for targets for teachers at the three upper pay spine levels. The reason for this is that in our work with schools, we are frequently asked about how to differentiate the measurement of the performance of this group of teachers.

Sample leadership related performance management objectives for UPS teachers (differentiated)

UPS 1 – For example, someone who is the post holder for one from the following:

Subject Leader; ECT mentor.

Sample subject leadership PM objective:

The UPS 1 teacher will lead the subject (name) across the whole school in an effective manner, in order that it is delivered by all teachers in an inspiring and innovative manner, by July 2025.

Success criteria:
- The leader, throughout the year, maintains effective communication of expectations.
- Teachers are well informed of subject priorities.
- Teachers feel confident in the delivery of the subject.
- Developmental support for teachers is provided throughout the year.
- Observation of exemplar provision by the subject leader is accessible throughout the year for others, (own class and other classes).

Sample ECT mentor PM objective:

The UPS 1 teacher will mentor an Early Career Teacher (ECT), in an effective manner, in order that the ECT becomes an effective teacher and team member by July 2025.

Resource bank reference 49

In carrying out performance management, senior leaders should reference the current National Teachers' Standards and their own in-house career progression grid. Our sample grid below is accessed through the resource bank, but we do, however, strongly suggest that headteachers work with all teaching staff to create their own bespoke model that recognises the context of the school.

Teachers' Standards 2012	Band 1 – Early stages	Band 2 – Developing	Band 3 – Accomplished	Band 4 – Becoming expert	Band 4 – Expert
Career grade – by year end	M1-M2	M3-M4	M5-M6	UPS 1	UPS3
Level of support for teacher	With support and mentoring:	Independently:	Starting to support others e.g. ITT students	Significant support of others	Proactive significant support of others and greater accountability
FOCUS AREA	Focus: Own class	Focus: Year Group	Focus: Whole School	Focus: Within/beyond school	As UPS1
1.1 Set high expectations which inspire, motivate and challenge pupils	Create and maintain a positive learning environment to promote teaching and learning. Know the curriculum at year group level. Establish expectations and sufficient challenge to ensure progress by setting appropriate goals and targets to stretch and challenge pupils at all levels. Ensure consistency in expectations of behaviour expected by all pupils in the class.	M3: Provide support and advice within the context of own year group/phase making sure that good practice is identified and shared. Support less experienced colleagues in setting goals and targets. M4: Provide support and advice beyond own year group/phase e.g. through planning and leading staff INSET. Act as role models for behaviour for all pupils and staff within the phase/year group.	M5: Develop the skills of others, particularly ITT students, to enable them to be able to inspire, motivate and challenge. M6: Have a significant impact on the work of others to improve teaching across the school. Ensure that all pupils in year group/phase/subject have appropriate goals to challenge and stretch at all levels.	Take an active part in setting goals across the school and possibly beyond, to stretch and challenge pupils of all backgrounds, skills and abilities. Take an active role in monitoring different elements of school life, for example, lead learning walks and give feedback to ensure consistency in subjects/environments etc. Provide feedback to SLT relating to areas of responsibility; initiate the creation of action	Support others to address any issues relating to learning environment; suggest actions and report to SLT Closely monitor the effectiveness of progress goals. Inform SLT of impact of monitoring. Uphold and articulate, as necessary, values, attitudes behaviours and culture of the school to the whole school community.

Career progression grid

Resource bank reference 52

This career progression grid is designed to enable individual teachers to evidence their career development against the current National Teachers' Standards to support their performance management process.

The focus areas are the eight standards taken directly from the National Teachers' Standards document.

The descriptors, divided into five career-stage blocks, enable teachers to see both the stage at which they are currently working, and to look ahead to their next steps. The intention is that each stage is iterative, i.e. teachers build upon each earlier stage as they progress their career. Individual schools may wish to add additional information into the descriptor boxes to meet their own contexts. We devised this resource after consultation with many school leaders who have helped us to differentiate the different stages. Our model is one we created for training – it is not 'union approved'. Every school is different, and no single set of expectations can be created that will work in all settings. To be as effective as possible, headteachers should develop their model to fit their own context but might find this useful as a skeleton to build upon.

In some of the focus areas, it is impossible to split a descriptor into individual one-year steps, but most have been divided into smaller steps. In practice, teachers annotate the grid and bring it along, with their portfolio of evidence, to support the discussions around their performance management.

This resource should be used alongside the full National Teachers' Standards document to ensure that appropriate judgements are made,

 # REFLECTIONS

- ∞ Performance management or management of performance?
- ∞ The application of a transparent career progression grid will enable teachers to understand what is expected of them at each stage of their career.

 # RESOURCES

Resource 48
A PowerPoint presentation on supporting the PM process for teaching staff.

Resource 49
Teachers – sample differentiated upper pay spine objectives.

Resource 50
Sample generic teacher objectives.

Resource 51
Teachers' standards overview.

Resource 52
Teacher career progression grid.

Headteacher appraisal

 **HOW**

Governors have a key role in helping to determine the strategic direction of the school as an organisation. This is an integral part of managing the headteacher performance process, in order to establish internal and external accountability. The headteacher performance management cycle should follow clear procedures and pay close attention to the ways that personal and professional goals mesh with school needs. Setting, monitoring, and reviewing objectives should make use of appropriate sources of information. Formal interim monitoring consists not only of monitoring progress against school performance objectives but provides an opportunity to take stock of the individual performance of the headteacher against the full range of their objectives.

The External Adviser (EA)

Crucial to the effectiveness of this process is the appointment of a suitably qualified and credible external adviser. This person can play an important role in mediating between individual needs of the headteacher and overall school goals, as well as working to help the governing body develop its capacity to carry out effective performance management.

The breadth and precision of the headteacher's objectives, the quality of performance information and productive engagement of stakeholders reflect the experience, maturity and quality of overall management processes within the school. It is important to note that the external adviser is not directly involved on decisions relating to pay.

It may be, however, that if an EA undertakes several reviews at different schools, he/she may have comparative experiences that can offer a voice of experience to governors. Governors may therefore seek advice, in principle, about potential pay awards, but not in detail.

Key questions

Questions to be considered by appointed governors involved in the performance management process for and with the headteacher include:

- ∞ Who is responsible for the implementation, preparation, and completion of headteacher performance management?
- ∞ What are the necessary competences of governors to develop and carry out headteacher performance management effectively?
- ∞ Within the panel of appointed governors, is there appropriate experience and expertise to carry out headteacher performance management in a rigorous and systematic way? If not, how can this be obtained?
- ∞ How do appointed governors make use of external support, especially the external adviser? Is the external adviser appropriately experienced and independent to ensure that governors are being provided with the best advice and support?
- ∞ Is there a suitable succession plan in place to ensure continuity or evolution of the process, i.e. new governors training to join the panel when experienced ones step down?
- ∞ How can appointed governors make best use of results e.g. governing body evaluation to identify areas of difficulty to enable them to refine, adapt and innovate headteacher performance management procedures?
- ∞ What training, mentoring and other capacity building is needed to use results effectively by appointed governors?

Key features

The implementation of effective headteacher performance management, (appraisal) process is characterised by:

- ∞ The integration with the school improvement plan and the performance management of all staff.
- ∞ A secure annual cycle of setting and reviewing objectives, together with interim monitoring.
- ∞ It being underpinned by sound relationships, characterised by openness, trust and integrity, among all those involved.
- ∞ It involves the setting of meaningful and challenging but achievable objectives for the headteacher.

∞ Striking an appropriate balance among internal and external accountability, development, and reward.

∞ Making use of evidence from a range of sources to inform decision-making.

∞ Being evaluated and adapted over time to meet evolving requirements of individual circumstances and shifting school needs within a dynamic context of governance.

∞ Ensuring it is appropriate for the stage of development of the school and the headteacher.

∞ Viewing it as part of an on-going and wider process of working with the headteacher and all staff to ensure high levels of performance.

∞ Ensuring it is integral to the development of overall governing body capacity to meet the needs of the school.

∞ Effective headteacher performance management is an attribute of highly effective governance.

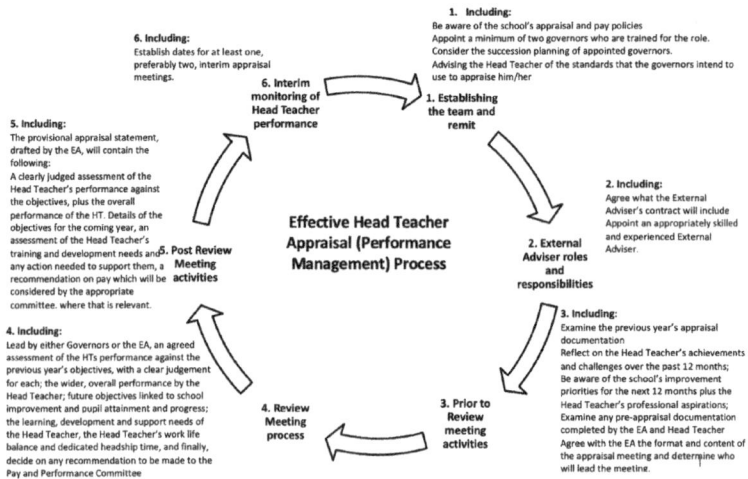

Model of the *headteacher performance management process cycle*
Resource bank reference 53

In addition to the details provided on the flow chart, the review process should contain the following key elements.

Setting Objectives

Department for Education regulations state 'the objectives set must be such that, if they are achieved, they will contribute to improving the education of the pupils at that school, and the implementation of any plan of the governing board designed to improve that school's educational provision and performance.'

Objectives should be set which are linked to school improvement and pupil achievement and progress. These should be SMART:

- ∞ Specific
- ∞ Measurable
- ∞ Achievable
- ∞ Relevant
- ∞ Time-bound

Objectives may be revised during the year if the school's or headteacher's circumstances change.

Identifying training, development, and well-being needs

Support, training, and development needs and how they will be addressed must be decided at the appraisal meeting. The headteacher's professional development should be linked to and support school improvement priorities and contribute to the achievement of appraisal objectives. The headteacher should play an active role in his/her professional development.

Governors have a duty of care for their headteacher. Attending to work-life balance issues and ensuring the well-being of the headteacher is well provided for is an essential part of the appraisal review discussions.

Monitoring, review, and support

Appraisal meetings should take place more than once a year. The governors and headteacher should engage in at least one, (preferably two), appraisal review meetings during the academic year to ensure regular professional dialogue. Several schools have termly review meetings.

The headteacher's salary review

The process for determining the remuneration of the headteacher must be fair and transparent. Governors should assure themselves that appropriate arrangements for linking appraisal to pay are in place and can be applied consistently, and that pay decisions can be objectively justified.

The School Teachers Pay and Conditions Document states "sustained high quality of performance having regard to the results of the most recent appraisal carried out on (date), should give the individual an expectation of progression up the pay range".

Before any recommendation to the Pay and Performance Committee on headteacher salary progression, appraisal governors need to have conducted research into the headteacher's current salary position within the context of the size of school.

A vital document to scrutinise is the 'School Teachers' Pay and Conditions Document' (STPCD). Governors should pay particular attention to the section titled 'Leadership Group Pay'. Paragraph 11.2 page 18 from the 2023 edition.

Examples of well worded objectives

The extract below shows examples of well-worded objectives for aspects of the headteacher's practice and responsibility. The full set can be found at resource bank reference 54.

Aspect of Leadership	Objective wording	Success Criteria
	1. The Head Teacher will implement processes and strategies across the school that ensures the relative attainment of pupils at the end of each key stage, and within each corresponding year group, is in line with the targets agreed, for all core subjects.	• Pupils at the end of EYFS and KS1 attain at least as well as their national peers in all subjects, (EYFS - 75% GLD, Y1 phonics – 80%, KS1 – Reading 78% with 25% at GD, Writing – 70% with 15% GD, Maths – 75% with 20% GD) • End of KS2 outcomes are in line with target set of 71% at age related expectations, and 10% at greater depth in combined subjects. (Reading – 80% with 15% GD, Writing – 87% with 18% GD, Maths – 80% with 18% GD) • Pupils make appropriate progress to enable them to attain well. • Strategies to enhance attainment by key groups of pupils across the school are embedded and consistent. • Staff members respond positively to new strategies and these contribute directly to improved outcomes.

The extract below shows how a single document can be both the precursor to the review meeting, the basis for discussions at the review meeting and subsequently become the draft appraisal review statement that confirms the agreements, decisions, and details from the review meeting.

Objective 1

The Executive Head Teacher will further embed processes and strategies across the two schools, that ensures the relative achievement of pupils, at the end of each Key Stage, and within each corresponding year group, is at least in-line with the national standards of 2019, by July 2023.

Success Criteria:
- Clear action plans are in place to achieve the objective, with measurable milestones throughout the year.
- Staff are fully aware of how to enhance pupil outcomes and demonstrate this consistently throughout the year.
- Strong progress towards agreed targets is evident throughout the year.
- Attendance is high in both schools, enabling learning to be consistent.

Head Teacher evidence: (brief summary of outcomes provided by HT prior to review meeting)
- RAP documents for School A which were monitored by the LA until the school became an academy
- End of KS2 SATs data show an upward trend in both schools; School A – in line with national with reading/writing and GPS. below national in maths and combined but significant improvement from previous year. School B – above national in writing – below in maths, reading and GPS – but 3 EHCP pupils in class with 2 children disapplied.
- EYFS – both schools above national in all areas
- Y1 Phonics – School A – increase to 64% from 49% - working with English Hub in this area and they were happy with the consistency in phonics teaching in both classes. 7/8 children who retook the phonics test passed. School B – 85% - 3 out 4 children who retook the phonics test passed.
- End of KS1 assessments at ARE all inline or above national in all areas at both schools but no children at the higher standard apart from 1 child at School A in reading.
- Improvement in pupil's focus and being ready to learn at School A
- Attendance lower that 95% in both schools – impacted by several children who have been school refusers. Working with families/FSW/outside agencies to address this.
- Staff working together to support each other is strong across both schools.

Decision (from review meeting): The objective has been well met.

Comments from reviewers:
The reviewers noted the clear enthusiasm the Executive Head Teacher has for taking on the challenge of Executive Headship. She has achieved much in both academies and has made some great appointments. Sarah has developed the teams and has generated a sense of togetherness across the two academies.

An example of the appraisal review document
Resource bank reference 55

REFLECTIONS

∞ Carefully managed headteacher appraisal is an opportunity for genuine reflection for the headteacher and governors. It should be seen as an important opportunity to review performance and is one aspect of headteacher accountability.

∞ Objectives that are crafted to meet the current identified priorities of both the headteacher and the school, will result in time efficient school improvement.
∞ One sometimes overlooked element of the headteacher appraisal is the opportunity for governors to consider headteacher well-being and how this can be supported.

 # RESOURCES

Resource 53
Model of the headteacher appraisal process.

Resource 54
Examples of headteacher objectives.

Resource 55
Headteacher appraisal blank documentation.

Resource 56
Headteacher standards with examples of evidence.

Evaluating the impact of continuing professional development (CPD)

 **WHY**

To evaluate the impact of professional development it is crucial to consider what was intended to be achieved, and what impact could reasonably be expected, in any given time frame.

The principles set out below recognise that impact should be considered in its widest sense – in terms of the needs of the school, the children, and the individual's professional development, whilst accepting that the weightings given to these different needs will not necessarily be consistent across all professional development activities.

The evidence base for impact evaluation needs to be broad. For instance, it could include enjoyment of learning or improvements in children's attitudes to schoolwork.

The evaluation of impact is not the end of the process but a crucial link between the development activities completed, and what may follow as part of the long-term planning for CPD.

Linked to the principles for effective evaluation of impact there are suggestions for questions to consider and discuss before the development activities are agreed, and after they have been completed.

The questions assume that individuals will be able to engage in professional dialogue with key school personnel as an element of their ongoing performance management process. The accompanying tools provide prompts and formats for recording the questions and answers.

 **HOW**

Principles underlying the effective evaluation of the impact of CPD

- ∞ Planning for CPD and the evaluation of its impact should be integral to the school's performance management process.
- ∞ Impact evaluation should focus on what participants learn, how they use what they have learned, and the effect this has on pupils' learning and their achievement.
- ∞ There should be an agreed timeline for evaluating outcomes, accepting that some outcomes, such as the improved performance by pupils, may take longer to become evident than others. Unanticipated outcomes will also be considered by the review.

- ∞ Planning and implementation of the impact evaluation should be a collaborative process between the individual and key staff involved in performance management and/or coaching and mentoring.
- ∞ The evidence base and the success criteria for the evaluation of impact should be agreed.
- ∞ Impact evaluation should be considered in the short, medium, and long term. Longer-term professional development activities should involve formative reviews of impact at agreed stages.
- ∞ The evaluation of impact should include a cost-benefit analysis of the professional development.
- ∞ The processes for evaluating the impact of CPD activities need to be reviewed regularly to ensure that they are effective and proportionate.

Definitions of Professional Development

Professional development within schools and academies takes many forms. For school leaders to evaluate and log the impact of intentional development, they need to have a working understanding of the different types of professional development.

In all cases the intent is for the participant to enhance either their skills, knowledge or understanding through the professional development opportunity and frequently all three aspects.

CPD type	Method and example	Knowledge impact	Skills impact	Understanding impact
Briefing				
Leadership Development Programme				
Subject specialism				
Update training.				
Qualification based.				

Resource bank reference 57

Professional development within schools and academies takes many forms. In order for school leaders to evaluate and log the impact of intentional development, they need to have a working understanding of the different types of professional development.

In all cases, the intent is for the participant to enhance either their skills, knowledge or understanding through the professional development opportunity and frequently all three aspects.

Questions to guide the evaluation of impact from CPD.

This appendix contains questions for the individual undertaking CPD, their line manager, and the person responsible for leading CPD within the school. The questions are based on the underlying principles. They are designed specifically for evaluating impact on the assumption that the preliminary needs identification and planning have already been carried out. If these questions are used in the context of performance management, it is important to stress the supportive and developmental nature of the process.

Stage of the process	Participant	Line manager/mentor/coach	CPD Leader
Prior to the CPD - These are questions to be considered before the professional development is undertaken.	Who have you discussed the potential impact of your intended learning outcomes with?		Is the strategy and timescale for evaluating impact appropriate?
	What specific outcomes will result from this professional development activity?		Has the activity been costed, and does the expected impact suggest that the professional development is cost-effective?
	How will your practice be changed?		How will the impact evaluation feed into performance management procedures?
	How will the professional development benefit you?		Is there more the school could do to maximise the impact?
	How will the professional development benefit the wider school, your colleagues, and children and young people?		

Questions to guide the evaluation of impact from CPD
Resource bank reference 58

This resource provides a structured set of questions for the individual undertaking CPD, their line manager, and the person responsible for leading CPD within the school. The questions are based on the underlying principles.

They are designed specifically for evaluating impact on the assumption that the preliminary needs identification and planning have already been carried out.

If these questions are used in the context of performance management, it is important to stress the supportive and developmental nature of the process.

Dialogue prompts for evaluating the impact of CPD
Teacher's dialogue prompts
Expected outcomes established
The expected impact of my CPD will be …
a) on pupils
b) on colleagues
c) on me
d) on the school as a whole

A guide for the dialogue about the impact of CPD
Resource bank reference 59

This guide is intended as a prompt for individual teachers, their line managers and the school's CPD leader to base dialogues on, in order to establish accurate reflection and the gathering of evidence that the planned CPD is making a difference in line with the principles above.

 **REFLECTIONS**

∞ Recognising the different types of professional development experience.
∞ Establishing the rationale underpinning the professional development experience.
∞ Clarification of expectations associated with professional development experiences.
∞ Gaining understanding of the importance of evaluating the impact of professional development experiences – what is the difference being made?

 # RESOURCES

Resource 57
Definitions of professional development.

Resource 58
Questions to guide the evaluation of impact from CPD.

Resource 59
Dialogue prompts for evaluating impact of CPD.

Resource 60
Line Manager's dialogue prompts for discussion.

Resource 61
Professional development register.

Resource 62
DfE Standard for teachers' professional development (July 2016).

Resource 63
CPD policy – example.

To access **all the resources** in the **online resource bank** for a small one-off subscription just:

- ∞ email headshipmatters@proton.me or
- ∞ visit www.tinyurl.com/3vtzknpu or
- ∞ scan the QR code below

Coaching and Mentoring Matters

**WHY**

The power of coaching has been recognised for many years. Astute headteachers see coaching skills as a vital addition to their leadership toolbox. So precisely what is it and how are these skills developed by headteachers and other leaders?

John Whitmore in his excellent book "Coaching for performance – growing people, performance and purpose", quotes the Concise Oxford Dictionary definition of the verb to coach as to "*tutor, train, give hints to, prime with facts*". He continues with "*This does not help us much, for those things can be done in in many ways some of which bear no relationship to coaching. Coaching is as much about the way these things are done as about what is done. Coaching delivers results in large measure because of the supportive relationship between coach and coachee, and the means and style of communication used.*

The coachee does acquire the facts not from the coach but from within himself, stimulated by the coach. Of course, the objective of improving performance is paramount, but how that is best achieved is what is in question."

Whitmore's central scaffold for any coaching conversation is what he calls the GROW model or sometimes adapted to become the T-GROW model, (a template of which can be found in the resource bank, reference 66).

T – the topic or issue for discussion, for example "the ways in which I could manage the behaviour of a small group of boys in my class".

G – the goal to be achieved, particularly in terms of the session time frame. For example, what is it you would like to have achieved by the time we conclude in 45 minutes time?

R – the "current reality" i.e. "what is going on with regard to this issue and what have you tried so far?" This is where the coachee provides the coach with a brief description of the context and the attempt(s) made so far to address the issue.

O – the options or possible strategies to be considered for implementation. This is where the conversation rests for most of the time as it is here that the coach draws out from the coachee a selection of ways forward and explores each in turn, eventually settling on one which will be acted upon. This is a very creative stage in the conversation and by using powerful open-ended questions the coach will enable the coachee to decide upon their own way forward.

W – the "will" statement or commitment to action. Here the coach asks the coachee to simply state what they are going to do to address the issue. This is a verbal commitment to themselves and to the coach who can use this as the starting point for the next conversation.

It is important to recognise that this model can be used in any sequence, it doesn't have to follow the T-GROW sequence precisely. So, for example a coachee may start the conversation with something like, "I'm thinking of splitting that group of boys up and placing them on different tables". This is an option being explored. The coach may then say something like, "Okay, that sounds interesting, just help me understand what is going on at present with these boys and what have you tried already?" This is a contextual question where the "current reality" is being described.

It is critical to use a coaching approach at the most appropriate time, and when the coachee is most receptive. We often use two examples to highlight these aspects. The first is if we are in a training room with a group and the fire alarm sounds, you really wouldn't want me to ask, "How does that make you feel?" You would much prefer me to be pro-active and lead the way to the assembly point outside. Similarly, the person to be coached must be receptive to that approach. A teacher coming to you as headteacher, (as head of answers), with a specific request for advice about how to manage a particular challenge, will not be receptive to open ended "how" or "what" questions. He or she wants a specific response detailing what he or she should do, not a twenty-minute coaching conversation, exploring options.

 HOW

To support headteachers in introducing the concept of coaching in school, we have created a PowerPoint presentation, (resource bank reference 64).

The first step in establishing a coaching culture in school is to clearly distinguish the differences between coaching and mentoring. When we do this with groups of leaders in a training context, we ask for two volunteers to assist us. They stand facing the group, standing on an imaginary line that connects them. The trainer leading this practical demonstration labels one volunteer as his coach and the other as his mentor. For the purpose of this demonstration, both volunteers and the trainer are members of staff in the same imaginary school.

Extending the imaginary line beyond the mentor, and with the trainer standing in that position, he explains that well beyond the mentor are the technical experts we rely upon in life, such as the person we call to fix our washing machine. We don't need to know how they do it, just how to get hold of them. The trainer then walks to the other end of the spectrum to explain that well beyond the coach are the groups of people who just ask questions, for example counsellors.

The trainer returns to the two volunteers and stands next to his mentor and asks the group "what sort of issues would you go to your mentor with and what would you expect her to do with and/or for you?" We tease out the precise nature of the mentor/mentee professional relationship.

Often it is hierarchical, with the mentor having lots more experience, and usually being a line manager. The issues brought by the mentee would be operational ones seeking advice, suggestions, and solutions that the mentee could take away with him to try regarding the issue. The mentor has most airtime in this conversation and remains the owner of the solutions, advice, and suggestions.

The trainer then moves to stand next to his coach and asks the same question "what sort of issues would you go to your coach with and what would you expect her to do with and/or for you?" This time the trainer teases out the issue could be more practice related, such as how to deal with a misbehaving group of boys in his class.

The coach would then focus on establishing the current reality of the situation by asking the coachee to describe what is going on and what he has tried so far. Using open ended questions, the most powerful of which are those starting with "how" or "what", the coach asks the coachee what sort of solutions and strategies he thinks may work. Resisting the strong temptation to turn into a mentor, by offering suggestions, the coach must maintain silence whilst the coachee is thinking in response to a question.

One of the most difficult skills to master when becoming a coach is to remain silent, as research has shown that teachers leave just three seconds of silence before they answer their own question! The other difficult skill to master is to resist becoming a mentor and telling the teacher what he should do.

The coachee has most airtime in this conversation to the extent of 80%. The coach encourages solutions to come from the coachee by exploring options and possibilities. The final part of this coaching conversation is for the coachee to commit to action out loud. Doing this shows commitment to the coach and to himself.

Concluding this demonstration to show the differences between mentoring and coaching, the group of leaders is tasked to coach one another on a current and unresolved professional issue they are facing at present. For coaching to have lasting impact, it must always be "real" and owned by the coachee, not artificial.

So, what are the skills required to coach effectively?

∞ **Listening** - When growing up we received formal education on reading and writing but not how to listen. Yet when it comes to education, and getting the very best from others, listening is probably one of the most important skills to have. If as a headteacher or senior leader you take on the role of coach, you need to learn to listen with real focus, suspending all your judgements and opinions. You also need to be listening not just to the words but also to the non-verbal signals such as body language. When we deliver coaching training, we always stress the importance of active listening, ensuring the coachee has 80% airtime, leaving the coach with just 20%. For many headteachers and senior leaders, keeping quiet is a real challenge!

∞ **Questioning -** Most of us can ask questions. When coaching, you need to be using powerful questions. These are questions that are short, typically 7 words or less; are open rather than closed; deepen the learning of the person being coached and move the person forward towards a goal. The most powerful questions begin with "how" or "what" and we always stress the difficulties generated by a "why" question, as this can create a sense of judgement and accusation in the coachee. In the early stages of developing coaching skills, coaches frequently feedback that they are concentrating so hard on constructing the next question, they often miss some of what the coachee is sharing. Also, we stress the importance of becoming comfortable with silence. This is one of the most challenging aspects of being a coach. Asking a well-constructed open-ended question will generate deep thinking in the mind of the coachee. This will manifest itself through silence as they process their thoughts towards an eventual response. If the coach is uncomfortable with this silence and decides to break it with words, (and research states that teachers asking questions of pupils will endure silence for an average of three seconds, before they answer their own question), they break the deep-thinking process for the coachee, and with it the eventual outcome. We train coaches to place their fore finger over their lips to send themselves a physical message to remain silent. Once mastered, and their comfort with silence is established, this can be dispensed with. Silence is golden.

∞ **Constructively challenging** - Challenging constructively is about not holding back but at the same time not destroying the relationship. Many people associate coaching with helping, which clearly it is. At the same time if the coaching never rocks the boat, it just becomes another nice chat. Playing back contradictions is a great way of constructively challenging. For example, rephrasing what you have heard as coach either confirms the received message or allows the coachee to re-articulate what they wanted to convey. Strategies such as "let me just replay what I think I have heard and tell me if I have received the right message" will allow the coachee to correct, confirm or paraphrase their thinking process.

∞ **Holding to account** - Accountability is one of the most powerful aspects of coaching. It has been suggested that people have a 95% chance of achieving an objective when they have accountability in place. When someone gives a commitment to doing something and they know that they will be held to account, it drives them forward. How effective are you at holding people to account as a headteacher? This bias to action is the "will" element of the GROW model found within Whitmore's book.

∞ **Seeing different perspectives -** Have you ever found yourself in a situation where it feels like you are pinned into a corner and there is nowhere to go? If so, the chances are you were stuck in a perspective. When coaching, you need to be able to help the coachee to explore different perspectives, so that they can choose those that are most powerful. Exploring "options" that the coach has drawn out of the coachee constitutes the 'O' within the GROW model.

∞ **Encouraging and supporting** - Encouraging and supporting when coaching can be the difference between someone keeping going or giving up. Acknowledging another person is an incredibly powerful way of keeping them motivated.

∞ **Trusting and using intuition** - We all have a hunch about something from time to time. The chances are that you have probably started to analyse it and make it logical or not. When coaching, your intuition is a powerful tool. Throw it out if it might be of benefit. The worst that can happen is that it is off the mark.

∞ **Keeping the focus on your client** - When you are in the role of coach your focus needs to be 100% on your client and their agenda. What this means is putting all the attention on the client and keeping your own agenda out of the way.

These eight key skills can not only help you when coaching but also make you an even better manager or leader. Take time to assess where your strengths lie and where you need to develop.

As with any process in schools, it is always helpful to audit skills to identify next steps to improvement. We have created a coaching audit to use with staff, (resource bank reference 65).

Coaching Skills Audit

To what extent	Very High	Fairly High	Fairly Low	Very Low
Do I manage structured coaching sessions by: • Agreeing the agenda • Managing time • Reaching consensus • Maintaining the focus				
Do I demonstrate personal qualities through: • Showing a sense of humour • Empathy and rapport • Non-judgemental • Being supportive and engaged • Display honesty. • Show enthusiasm • Maintain optimism				
Do I use appropriate body language through: • Suitable posture • Sensitive eye contact • Reinforcing and affirming gestures • Showing open and positive, non-threatening, non-intimidating • Mirroring				
Do I question for understanding through: • Using open questions – what, when, where, who • Asking probing questions – how much, how often, how many				

 **CASE-STUDY**

Andrea, (not her real name), is a highly effective teacher who always establishes fantastic relationships with pupils. They all make great progress because of her consistently high level of effectiveness. In the classroom she is confident and sure of what she wants to achieve.

However, as public events such as the termly meeting with parents approached, Andrea would become increasing anxious, as she lacks confidence when talking with parents and other adults. She approached John, her headteacher, to share her anxiety in the hope he would be able to help her with her situation.

John suggested a series of coaching conversations with Jackie, an experienced coach he knew. Andrea agreed, and the first meeting was set in the diary.

Jackie worked with Andrea over a period of four weeks, using the GROW model from Whitmore's book "Coaching for performance", as the template for their discussions. They established the "goal", (G), for each session and Andrea related her current "reality", (R), regarding her perception of the meetings with parents. Most time in each session was exploring "options", (O), with Jackie carefully probing Andrea's thought process to generate as many options as possible. When Andrea selected one to explore still further, she stated to Jackie her intention to act, her "will", (W), statement.

At the start of the following session, Jackie would always ask how the actions went and the difference Andrea's latest strategy made to her confidence levels. Gradually, Andrea became more confident with parents and public occasions as she had developed a string of strategies to use during these events.

The power of coaching resulted in Andrea's anxiety levels being significantly reduced and she felt a greater level of confidence, almost matching that she continues to display in the classroom.

# REFLECTIONS

∞ Context and coachee must be conducive and open to coaching.
∞ Coaching skills take time and practice to become fully embedded.
∞ Silence is golden.
∞ GROW model enables a structured conversation.
∞ Coaching is a highly effective tool in the headteacher "toolkit".

# RESOURCES

Resource 64
A PowerPoint presentation on the coaching process.

Resource 65
Coaching audit

Resource 66
T-Grow template

Resource 67
Think piece – "Instructional coaching" Robbie Burns

# FURTHER READING

John Whitmore, "Coaching for performance – growing people, performance and purpose" Nicholas Brealey Publishing, 2004

Max Landsberg "The Tao of coaching", Profile Books Ltd, 2003

Dr Spencer Johnson "Who moved my cheese" Vermilion Press, 1999

To access **all the resources** in the **online resource bank** for a small one-off subscription just:

- ∞ email <u>headshipmatters@proton.me</u> or
- ∞ visit www.tinyurl.com/3vtzknpu or
- ∞ scan the QR code below

Shared Team Culture Matters

Establishing a positive school culture

**WHY**

Establishing and maintaining a consistent and positive culture that is upheld by all is a significant challenge for any headteacher. Culture is best defined as "the way we do things around here". It is a tangible feature that visitors to the school quickly become aware of. Achieving the desired culture is through establishing clarity of ethos, (based upon clearly defined values and expectations), and applying these in a consistent way, so that the culture becomes a distinctive and defining dimension of the school, lived out in daily practice.

Put simply: **Culture = Ethos + Consistent Practice**

One "litmus test" for evaluating the effectiveness of your school culture is when pupils join your school during the year and are rapidly assimilated into behaving in line with your school cultural expectations. Similarly, when new staff members join your team, they bring experiences from their former roles which may enhance your school practice, and these would need to be considered. Initially, however, they would need to adopt your practice to ensure consistency throughout the school.

This resource is designed to support headteachers and senior leaders to work proactively together to develop a positive school culture. There have always been references to culture or cultural development within the evolution of Ofsted's school inspection handbook, and have typically included phrases such as the following:

∞ Inspectors will consider whether leaders and governors have created a culture of high expectations, aspirations, and scholastic excellence in which the highest achievement in academic and vocational work is recognised …

∞ Responses to the staff questionnaire and Parent View will provide useful evidence for judging the culture that has been established in the school by leaders and managers …

∞ Inspectors will consider whether governors work effectively with leaders to communicate a vision, ethos and strategic direction of the school and develop a culture of ambition …

∞ Leaders and governors have created a culture that enables pupils and staff to excel…

∞ Leaders promote equality of opportunity and diversity exceptionally well, for pupils and staff, so that the ethos and culture of the whole school prevents any form of direct or indirect discriminatory behaviour …

∞ Leaders and managers have created a culture of vigilance where pupils' welfare is actively promoted…

∞ Leaders set high expectations of pupils and staff. They lead by example to create a culture of respect and tolerance…

∞ Leaders promote equality of opportunity and diversity, resulting in a positive school culture…

∞ The school's open culture actively promotes all aspects of pupils' welfare …

∞ Relationships among learners and staff reflect a positive and respectful culture.

∞ Leaders have created an open and positive culture around safeguarding that puts pupils' interests first.

We know that the school culture is something tangible and that there are certain cultural dimensions and qualities that are needed in any improving school. These include areas such as vision, trust, and resilience. There are also a wide range of cultures that support success. We recognise that this is not an exhaustive list but know, from working with many school leaders, that this is a helpful tool to support the systematic review and development of positive cultures.

 # HOW

We have developed a simple resource that is helpful in supporting school teams to talk about culture and how to develop this. We have created a series of culture card posters, (such as the one below), and each one has a spectrum with two extremes briefly described.

One example of a culture dimension (a total of thirteen), (resource bank reference 68):

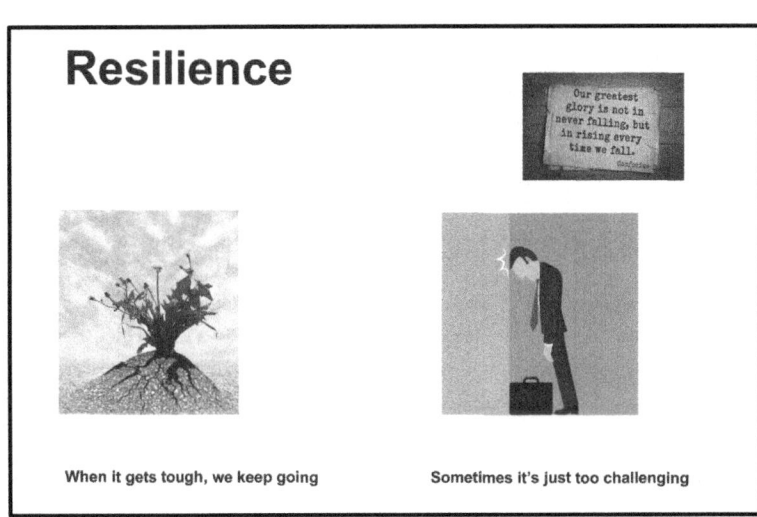

Our suggestion is that if you are wishing to initiate a discussion about culture, ask people, (anonymously if it helps, using post-it strips), to indicate where they feel the school is on the spectrum of each dimension. This provides a basic audit on which to build, and facilitate discussions along the lines of "what needs to change for us to move higher up the spectrum?"

We have also created a one-page evaluation/audit sheet replicating these cultures for headteachers and senior leaders to indicate whether they evaluate the dimension to be "emerging" "developing" or "established" and then, most importantly, to provide the evidence that confirms this judgement. See sample extract below.

Evaluation of cultural dimensions of the school (ethos)

Cultural dimension	Evidence	Emerging	Developing	Established
Aspiration 'Your aspirations are your possibilities'				
Clarity 'We have clear communication and straight-forward systems ensuring that we all understand our roles and responsibilities				
Consistency 'The right people in the right place doing the right things in the right ways.				
Courage 'We can do it'				
Curiosity 'We always seek new and better ways of doing things'				
Emotional intelligence 'We understand the importance of relationships'				
Judgement 'We make the right calls'				
Momentum 'We keep building on our best'				
Passion 'We are here for the children, always'				
Persuasion 'We are excellent communicators able to get our messages across'				

Evaluating the cultural dimensions of the school (ethos + practice)
Resource bank reference 69

 **CASE-STUDY**

Reflecting upon my ten years of headship at the same school, I can honestly say I have established the culture I firmly believe in. It hasn't been easy at times though. I inherited the headship, moving into the hotseat from being deputy headteacher, and prior to that the school's year six class teacher. So, I knew what I was taking on! And I knew what I wanted to change together with the rationale underpinning that direction of travel.

Ours is a faith-based school and I wanted to recalibrate and deepen the principles defining our ethos. I also wanted to embed a consistency of practice by staff and a consistency of experience for pupils.

To do this I knew I would have to "hold a mirror up" to the then current practice for others to see the gaps in our culture that I could see. Sometimes this came at a price and some members of staff chose to move on. Appointing my own staff reached a tipping point where I appointed more than I had inherited. This was the game changing moment for me. Now we really could get to grips with enhancing provision, practice and "the way we do things around here".

We had a Section 48 (denominational) inspection in 2015 and the school was judged to be outstanding in all areas. This was followed by a visit from Ofsted in 2017 which left us with the judgement of being a good school. I was pleased with both outcomes and became fully determined to have both judgements re-endorsed the next time around. More work on embedding our culture ensued!

Our next round of inspections, (2022), brought the outcomes I had been working for. We were reconfirmed as outstanding for RE, Collective Worship and Catholic Life, and in July 2022 Ofsted reconfirmed ours to be a good school.

I am proud of what we have achieved, and these are some of the positive words that inspectors used to describe our culture.

Section 48 Inspection 2022:

∞ Behaviour, in the classroom and around school, is exemplary. Pupils consistently demonstrate a warm appreciation of and care for each other as they all feel genuinely 'valued' and 'unique'.
∞ Pupils have a strong voice in the decision-making process; they say they are always listened to and their opinions appreciated so they are happy and secure in confidently expressing their views and feelings.
∞ Our Lady of Mount Carmel is a wonderful Catholic school. From the moment of entering the premises it is very clear that its prime purpose is Catholic education, helping children to develop their faith and to understand that God loves them. It is a most welcoming school where everyone is valued and respected and enjoys life to the full.

Ofsted Inspection 2022:

∞ Leaders have high expectations of what they want pupils to achieve. Pupils enjoy learning a broad curriculum. In lessons, pupils listen carefully. They work quietly and concentrate well. They are eager to contribute their ideas in lessons and know when the time is right to do so.

∞ Pupils told the inspector that they consider their school virtues, 'happy, caring, valued, unique, successful', in whatever they do at school. Pupils place importance on being kind and helpful. Older pupils are role models for the younger pupils. They help to serve them during lunchtimes, where they assist at the salad bar and help them to carry their trays.

Lindsay Shaw

Head Teacher, Our Lady of Mount Carmel Catholic Primary School, Doncaster

 REFLECTIONS

∞ Culture = Ethos + Consistent Practice
∞ Cultural audit and examination of perceptions across stakeholders and then draft a culture improvement plan.

The importance of team development and effectiveness

WHY

Organisations cannot function effectively without teams. Within a primary school there are multiple teams and people may have different roles within them. Groups develop into teams when their common purpose is understood by all of the members. In effective teams, each member plays an assigned role using his/her talents to the best advantage. When teams use their shared skills to accentuate strengths and minimise weaknesses, team objectives are usually achieved.

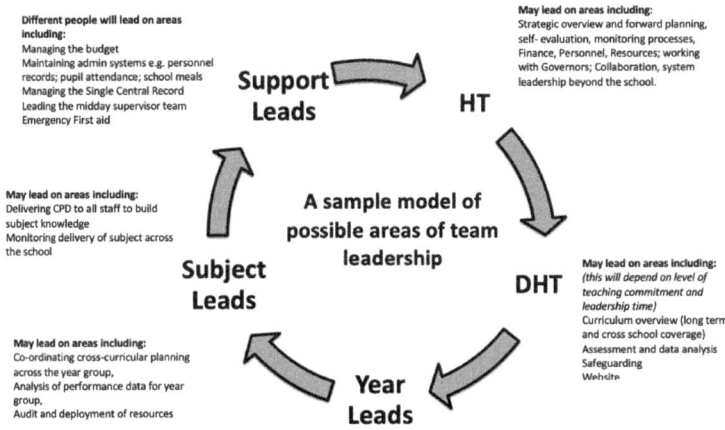

A model of possible areas of team leadership
Resource bank reference 70

For example, in this model we assume the deputy headteacher has a teaching role. He/she might be the team leader for assessment and the wider curriculum overview, but also a team member of the appropriate year group/phase team and subject team.

Every school is different and operates within a unique context. The diagram offers some possible ways of how some of the many different tasks in school might be allocated across a school. The number of variables, e.g. size, budget and staffing make it impossible to propose any fixed model.

Similarly, the "Year Leads" would take the lead role when working with their year team but would be a team member of many other teams. Within a school, there will be multiple teams with everyone belonging to several different teams. As individuals working in complex organisations, it is helpful for headteachers to analyse their teams to ensure that they are working effectively. Headteachers often choose to move different people around to widen their experience and each time staff change roles, new teams must develop. Regular review of a team's performance is key to continuous improvement and learning.

Team leaders need to be offered training to ensure that they get the most from their team. An understanding of how teams develop and the team leader role in supporting this is important for all team leaders. Successful teams are rarely created by chance or good luck – although many headteachers say to us, "I am lucky with my staff". We believe that luck plays little part in the creation of effective teams and that skilled leaders, who make the effort to know their staff and something of their individual motivations, tend to create and develop the best teams.

Effective teams have some specific characteristics:
- ∞ Have a clear sense of purpose.
- ∞ Set clear and demanding targets.
- ∞ Have lots of discussion in which everyone takes part.
- ∞ Have an honest and open atmosphere where people can express feelings and ideas.
- ∞ Make most decisions by agreement.
- ∞ Have members who all participate fully.
- ∞ Allow criticism which is frank and relatively comfortable – constructive.

We have created an audit to help identify strengths and areas of development within your teams.

An audit of some of the characteristics of effective teams

CHARACTERISTIC	TEAM 1			TEAM 2			TEAM 3			EVIDENCE
Evaluation	Em	D	Es	Em	D	Es	Em	D	Es	
We share an understanding of our objectives										
We are ambitious in setting our objectives										
There is a high level of trust and respect in the team										
We accept constructive criticism from team members										
We openly address any disagreements										
Team members are open and honest with each other										
All team members actively participate in the team										
The team leader facilitates discussion and does not dominate										
Different team members are able to lead as appropriate										
Discussions are focused and productive										

Extract from team audit - Resource bank reference 73

 **HOW**

This teamwork resource comprises a brief overview of how successful teams develop, based on the research by Bruce Tuckman, an audit of team effectiveness and some suggestions for motivating teams.

This theory was first proposed by psychologist Bruce Tuckman in 1965. It stated that teams would go through five stages of development: forming, storming, norming, performing and adjourning. These stages supposedly start when the group first meets and last until the project ends. Each of these rhyming stages are aptly named and plays a significant role in building a highly functioning business team.

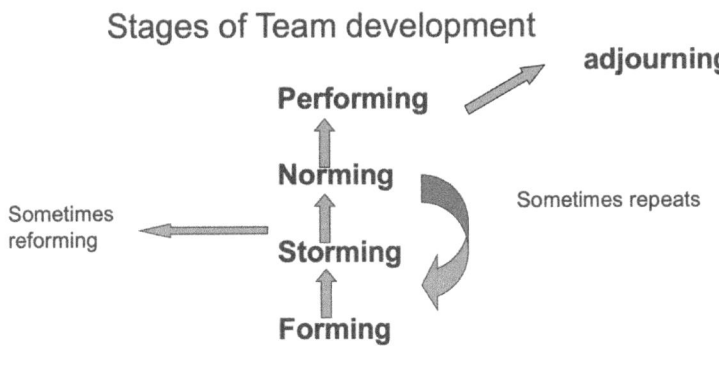

Bruce Tuckman

Resource bank reference 71

The five stages of team development

The first stage of team development is **forming.** The team members have just been introduced to each other and the and the specific task of school improvement has been allocated. This is an interesting psychological moment as team members tend to behave independently at this stage. Whilst there may be good spirits and good intentions, the trust won't necessarily be there yet.

During this stage of the team development, it's common to discuss:

∞ Everyone's skills, background, and interests.
∞ The project goal to be achieved.
∞ The timeline and how the team will achieve this goal.
∞ Ground rules, regulations, protocols, and sensitivities to be agreed and signed up to.
∞ What individual roles each member will play within the team.

It's important at this stage that the group starts to develop an understanding of the part each person will play.

The second stage of team development is **storming.** The storming stage is when the initial excitement and good grace has run out. The reality and the weight of completing the project has now most likely settled in.

This is the stage where egos may start to show themselves and tempers may flare. The team may disagree on how to complete a particular task or voice any concerns. At this stage, looking to a strong leader for guidance is vital. It is worth pointing out that some teams fail at this stage and new teams have to be created.

The third stage of team development is **norming.** This is the stage where things tend to settle down. Your team can get into the groove of working together towards a common goal. However, during the norming stage, there can be a few overlaps with storming.

As new tasks appear, there may still be some incidents of conflict. However, as you've already gone through the worst part, these disagreements may be easier to address.

The fourth stage of team development is **performing.** The performing stage is where your team can hit its stride. Each team member understands everyone's strengths and weaknesses and they are familiar enough with each other to help.

This is the stage where each member is confident and motivated. It's also where they can operate without strict supervision. Some teams don't make it to this stage, so if you do it's a real achievement. It's the stage that every group will hope to make as it's when you can get your best work done. When working in a supportive and cohesive team, creativity can be sparked, and team members will have high morale.

The final and fifth stage of team development is **adjourning.** It was only in 1977 that Tuckman added the fifth and final stage. When the project ends, the team will disband. If they have reached the performing stage, then there could be a sense of mourning if they have grown close. However, having positive shared experiences will make it easier if you work with some of these people again.

The Development of Successful Teams

All teams go through different stages of development as they mature. These stages are normal and to be expected. Many team leaders are surprised when the team enters the 'storming' phase. Ineffective teams may never get beyond this.

Various academics have created models of team development, one easily accessible one is the Bruce Tuckman model. For more reading and further development of the model, type 'Tuckman' into a search engine

Stage	Features	How it feels	Leader role
Forming	Goals identified; Limited input from team member Culture of politeness due to unfamiliarity Little agreement	Positive and polite, some anxiety as unclear about team goals etc. Uncertainty about roles Limited trust Checking each other out	Provide clear direction. Outline your expectations Set the group rules agreed by everyone Set objectives for the whole team and individual team members Get to know team members.
Storming	Potential challenge by team members, possible conflict Decisions hard to reach Morale may be low	Team may feel overwhelmed by task if it hasn't been clearly defined. Stressful Possible frustration. Little team spirit.	Clarify and reiterate processes, goals, roles etc Resolve conflicts Give support to those who are unsure Remain positive in the face of challenge Retain culture of honest, open communication to build trust

Resource bank reference 72

At different times in the development of teams, with reference to their stage of development, leaders will need to provide motivation to enable the team to continue to develop.

Some basic strategies for motivating team members and leading them effectively:

1. Get to know team members as individuals; seek out their strengths and support them to address weaknesses with relevant, high quality PD
2. Be 100% consistent i.e. don't favour certain team members or allow some team members to ignore the 'rules' e.g. meeting deadlines
3. Consult so that the team feel a shared ownership i.e. 'do with' and not 'do to'
4. Listen (and where appropriate, act on what you hear) to show the views of the team are important
5. Acknowledge and use specialist knowledge and skills in the team – this builds commitment and self esteem
6. Be sensitive to individuals i.e. know the approach that will work best with different people - the aim is not compliance but discretionary effort
7. Celebrate good news and achievements – success often creates further success
8. Give praise when it is due, but make sure it is sincere and deserved
9. Retain strong professional relationships that are caring and supportive, bearing in mind that sometimes a professional distance will be necessary in order to be objective

Some basic strategies for motivating teams
Resource bank reference 76

REFLECTIONS

- ∞ Organisations cannot function effectively without teams.
- ∞ Recognise and facilitate the stages of team development.
- ∞ Educate your team to understand the characteristics of each stage of team development.
- ∞ When the team membership changes, often it returns to the forming stage.

 # RESOURCES

Resource 68
Culture cards

Resource 69
Evaluation proforma to audit cultural dimensions in school.

Resource 70
Model of possible areas of team leadership.

Resource 71
Stages of team development (Tuckman).

Resource 72
The development of successful teams.

Resource 73
Audit of the characteristics of effective teams.

Resource 74
Characteristics of effective teams' notes.

Resource 75
Great schools card sort.

Resource 76
Strategies for motivating teams and leading them effectively.

Resource 77
Team development card sort (with answers!).

Resource 78
Carousel exercise to share experience/expertise/advice.

 # FURTHER READING

Andy Buck, "Leadership Matters 3.0" John Catt Educational Ltd, 2018

Andy Buck, "Honk" John Catt Educational Ltd, 2019

To access **all the resources** in the **online resource bank** for a small one-off subscription just:

- ∞ email headshipmatters@proton.me or
- ∞ visit www.tinyurl.com/3vtzknpu or
- ∞ scan the QR code below

Governance matters

At the time of writing, the DfE has just published two new governance guides:

- ∞ Maintained Schools Governance Guide
- ∞ Academy Trust Governance Guide

This non-statutory guidance replaces the governance handbook from 2019.

There are no new requirements for governors or trustees but headteachers should ensure that everyone on the board is aware of, and can access, the right guide for the school type.

You should also remove copies of, or reference to, the previous governance handbook in your board's files and documents.

As part of this review, the DfE has withdrawn the following documents:
- ∞ Governance Handbook
- ∞ Governance Competency Framework
- ∞ Clerking Competency Framework
- ∞ Governance Structures and Roles
- ∞ Statutory Policies for Schools and Academy Trusts

Much of the information in those documents is now covered in the new governance guides.

We have updated the resource bank to reflect the changes, particularly to the PowerPoint presentation to support governor training.

 **WHY**

In our experience, one of the areas of concern for many headteachers is working with governors to establish a solid relationship that enables governors to fulfil their statutory duties and have a positive impact on the school.

We must always remember that governors are volunteers and have many different motivations for taking on the role. Some governors are parents who feel that by becoming a governor, they will get an insight into their own children's education. This is a perfectly valid reason but may sometimes require tactful training to ensure that they understand that any issues or concerns pertaining to their own children are not suitable for discussion at governing body meetings. Many governors bring extensive and valuable skills to the role which they are selflessly willing to share to help the school thrive. Governors with expertise in areas such as accounting; human resources and law are invaluable. The most effective governing bodies are those which bring a mix of skills, insight and life experience to the role, each contributing something different that helps the school.

To be of maximum effectiveness, it is essential that roles and responsibilities are crystal clear and understood by the whole governing body. One of the best ways to ensure this, is regular governor training. One of the issues for some governing bodies is finding suitable training. There are organisations such as the National Governor Association (NGA) and sites such as 'The Key' for governors, which may provide answers to many questions. For maintained schools, training may be available through Local Authority sources and Trusts may have their own in-house training. We are often asked to deliver governor training sessions to schools during which we offer an overview of the role and a range of resources to support the governing body in carrying out their core functions.

For our generic training, we have created a governance pack, based on many years of delivering basic governor training in schools. Our governor training resources are intended to use to support governors in their role. Our suggestion is that these resources can be kept in a governor file, accessible to all governors, enabling governors to demonstrate their effectiveness and understanding of the role.

Our belief is that these governing body training sessions should ideally be run annually for all governors to attend. Our resource bank enables headteachers to deliver this training themselves. The benefits of in-house training are firstly cost, and secondly permanent access to the training.

 **HOW**

Training resources

Our first resource is a generic set of PowerPoint slides that can be adapted to the individual school circumstances, (resource bank reference 79). The response from governing bodies who have used this, is that it has given confidence in understanding the role and the expectations of governors. Areas in a red font are those that the school should personalise with their own information.

The title of the slide set is 'Update training' but the initial slides, (which can be deleted if required), relate to governing body preparation for inspection as that is often the time when we get most requests for this type of training.

The areas covered in the slide set are:
∞ Preparing for inspection.
∞ The role of governors and revisiting the three core functions.
∞ The impact of the governing body.

∞ Creating a governance improvement plan.
∞ Skills audits.
∞ Content suggestions for a governing body folder.
∞ Some questions and answers for governors to consider.

If preparing the governing body for inspection, slides 2-5 need personalising to the school.

Slide 6 states what inspectors are looking for and is useful to any governing body update.

Slide 7 lists the three core functions of the governing body, reworded in the new March 2024 governance guide.

Slides 8-10 take each core function, providing a little more detail, and asks the key question, 'how have you held the headteacher/senior leadership team to account' in this particular area.

Slides 11-14 relate to governing body impact, with a practical exercise to capture this, which we suggest is done on an annual basis.

Slide 15 is an example of one area of a governing body improvement plan.

Slide 16 references the removal of the former governance competency framework but suggests that the pre-2024 skills audit we created might still be useful.

Slide 17 identifies some possible next steps to establish effective governance.

Governor skills audit and training plan

The DfE 'Competency Framework for Governance', published in 2017, was a twenty-seven-page document detailing sixteen competencies underpinned by a foundation of principles and personal attributes.

The sixteen competencies were grouped into six features namely,
∞ Strategic leadership
∞ Accountability

∞ People
∞ Structures
∞ Compliance
∞ Evaluation.

With the introduction of the new governance guide in March 2024, this document has been removed and not yet replaced. It suggests that *"the governing body can evaluate the effectiveness of their governance through a combination of self-assessment tools, independent perspectives and skills audits"*, (para: 6.1) but there is no direct signposting to these.

The governance guide states that:

"Regular evaluation to monitor and improve the quality and impact of governance by:

> ∞ *completing regular skills audits, aligned to the school's strategic plan, to identify skill and knowledge gaps and inform:*
> > o *recruitment needs*
> > o *training and development plans*
> > o *induction of new governors, including training on KCSIE and keeping pupils safe online in education*
> ∞ *regularly reviewing the governing body effectiveness, how well governors work together and governors' performance and their participation in discussions*
> ∞ *commissioning external reviews to get an independent assessment of the governing body's effectiveness and areas for development, particularly at key growth or transition points*
> ∞ *following legal requirements for document retention and accurately documenting:*
> > o *evidence of the governing body and its committee's discussions and decisions*
> > o *any evaluation of the governing body's impact"*

It also states specific skill sets are needed by at least one member of the governing body relating to areas including interpretation of performance data and finance.

In terms of training, it says that 'effective governors undertake training where needed' and that Local Authorities are obliged to secure the provision of training to governors under Section 22 of the Education Act 2022.

Finally, it clarifies that:

"A governing body is responsible for:

- ∞ *allocating a governance training and development budget*
- ∞ *identifying appropriate induction and ongoing development requirements*
- ∞ *providing an induction for new governors, associate members and the governance professional identifying specific training such as safeguarding, Prevent, and how to keep pupils safe online, ensuring that all governors and the governance professional have read and follow Part 2 of Keeping Children Safe in Education guidance*
- ∞ *encouraging everyone on the governing body and the governance professional to develop their knowledge and skills"*

As the new document has only just been published, we assume that further resources may become available. We have, however, decided to keep our own skills audit in the resource bank as it may still prove useful to some governing bodies.

Our concise three-page document addresses all of the former competencies but also enables governors to self-evaluate their level of confidence with each competency on a best-fit model.

There is no statutory requirement for governors to undertake a skills audit, but in using it, boards will be able to demonstrate how effectively they take the responsibility for the improvement in effectiveness of the board.

Governor's self-perception of the 6 features of effective governance	Descriptor	1	2	3
1.Strategic Leadership	*'Effective boards provide confident, strategic leadership to their organisations; they lead by example and 'set the tone from the top'. These competencies relate to the core function of boards to set vision ethos and strategic direction.'*			
1a: Setting direction. *'The knowledge and skills required for effectiveness in setting the strategic direction of the organisation, planning and prioritising, monitoring progress and managing change.'*	Has a good understanding of national and local education policy and issues. Is able to apply this knowledge to the school's strategic priorities and understands the Governor role in contributing towards setting direction Offers appropriate challenge to the SLT to ensure that changes are in the best interests of children and the school. Can articulate strategic goals of the school to others and explain reasons for, and benefits of change.			
1b: Culture, values, and ethos *'The knowledge and skills required to set, demonstrate and monitor culture, values and ethos of the organisation.'*	Has a good understanding of the ethos and values of the school and were involved in setting and monitoring these within the school. Understands how the Code of Conduct for the Board embodies the culture, values and ethos of the school. Models the culture, values and ethos in the role of Governor.			
1c: Decision making. *'Effective decision-making is about moving from free and frank discussion to specific, measurable actions.'*	Able to identify viable options for the context of the school that will enable the school to achieve its' goals. Acts with the highest degree of impartiality and integrity in decision making and stands by the agreed decisions of the Board.			
1d: Collaborative working *'Effective Boards enable productive relationships.'*	Can identify key stakeholders and is proactive in consulting and responding to their views. Uses clear language to communicate with parents, pupils, staff and the local community. Is credible, open and honest with stakeholders and considers the impact of the board's decisions on them.			

Extract from the governor skills audit
Resource bank reference 80

Our suggestion is that the skills audit is carried out annually and the results collated which then identifies any training needs for the year.

Board training plan based on the outcomes of the skills audit.
Based on the former Competency Framework for Governance

The core functions of the governing body include, but are not limited to ensuring:

- that the vision, ethos, and strategic direction of the school are clearly defined.
- that the headteacher performs their responsibilities for the educational performance of the school
- the sound, proper and effective use of the school's financial resources

Governor's self-perception of the 6 features of effective governance	Training needs
1.Strategic Leadership *'Effective boards provide confident, strategic leadership to their organisations; they lead by example and 'set the tone from the top'. These competencies relate to the core function of boards to set vision ethos and strategic direction.'*	
1a: Setting direction. 1b: Culture, values, and ethos 1c: Decision making. 1d: Collaborative working 1e: Risk management	
2. Accountability for educational standards and financial performance. *'These are the competencies that the Board needs in order to deliver its core functions of holding Executive Leaders to account for the educational and financial performance of the organisation.'*	
2a: Educational improvement 2b: Rigorous analysis of data 2c: Financial frameworks and accountability 2d: Financial management and monitoring 2e: Staffing and performance management 2f: External accountability	

Extract from the governor training plan proforma
Resource bank reference 81

Governing body improvement plan

There is no statutory requirement for governing bodies to have an improvement plan, but our experience is that many governing bodies feel that it is useful in identifying their own next steps for improvement. Within our online resource bank, we have created a generic plan that can be used to support the governing body in writing their annual plan, (reference 82).

We have a proforma to support the governing body in creating a very brief plan – our model is two sides of a single piece of paper. Our suggestion is that any areas for improvement are captured against the three core functions of the governing body in an action plan, identifying the action, the intended impact and then the practical aspects of who will do it? when will it be done? how will it be done?

Area 1: Ensuring that the vision, ethos and strategic direction of the school are clearly defined.

Actions	Who	When	How	Intended Impact
GB have a clear view of the progress of the new School Improvement Plan and proactively track the issues that have been identified for improvement by staff/governors	FGB	Throughout the year, at GB meetings and when visiting the school	Updates at all termly GB meeting; written feedback from relevant staff appended to all Action Plans, shared with GB at meetings	Governors provide a balance of challenge and support to leaders, understanding the strengths and areas of development of the schools
Governing body to be well prepared for inspection.	FGB	Throughout the year, at GB meetings and when visiting the school	Governors to ensure they are fully aware of their three core functions.	Governors can articulate the strategic direction, strengths, and areas of development of the school. Governors can describe their first-hand experiences from time spent in school and with staff.

Extract from the generic governing body improvement plan
Resource bank reference 82

How governors can demonstrate impact

Governors need to be able to demonstrate that their work has an impact on the school. This needs to go far beyond attendance at meetings. Governors need to be able to discuss the experience of pupils, staff and parents. What is it like to be a pupil or a member of staff at the school? What do parents think about the school?

From an inspection perspective, one of the ways that the governing body can demonstrate impact is through the governing body minutes from meetings. Minutes of meetings indicate where governors are challenging the school's headteacher/senior leaders' judgements, particularly around pupils' progress and the quality of education; an appropriate level of knowledge about the school curriculum; an awareness of national data and how children compare nationally plus a clear understanding of finances. Accurate minutes from meetings are essential and employing a professional clerk helps governors to demonstrate their impact.

A governing body file containing some of the earlier suggestions such as a collated skills audit and related training plan and a governing body Improvement plan supports evidence of impact.

A practical activity that we often use with governors is to ask them to capture, on post-it notes, everything they can think of that demonstrates impact. These are collected onto a large board divided into the five inspection areas. Once governors have offered all their suggestions, the post-its are collated into a document and the examples of impact are matched to the three core functions.

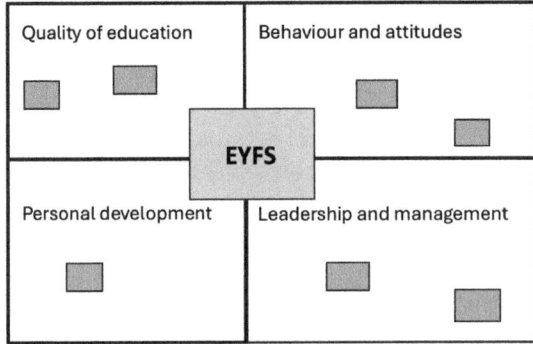

What impact on each of the 5 inspection areas can Governor's evidence?

Our aim is to demonstrate what Governors have seen with their own eyes and heard with their own ears, not simply what they have been told. Governors are committed to fulfilling their core functions:

The core functions of the governing body include, but are not limited to ensuring:
1 the vision, ethos and strategic direction of the school are clearly defined.
2. the headteacher performs their responsibilities for the educational performance of the school
3. the sound, proper and effective use of the school's financial resources.

Quality of Education	• Governors have met regularly with different members of staff e.g. following Learning walks, to deepen the Governors understanding of specific aspects of teaching, learning and assessment and to monitor issues such as learning behaviours. (Core Function 2) • Governors regularly have classroom visits to improve their knowledge of teaching and learning and also have 'walkabouts' to look at aspects such as the learning environment (Core Function 2) These are all in line with the agreed policy and protocols for Governor visits. • The Governor with responsibility for assessment meets every half term with DHT to discuss progress and attainment with a focus on the attainment of specific pupil groups. • The Governor with responsibility for EYFS meets with the EYFS Lead and reports back to the full GB • Termly assessment reports are presented to the GB (Core Function 2) • Governors are regularly updated on pupil outcomes. They compare data over time to identify trends and have an appropriate awareness of the performance of the schools in relation to all schools nationally. (Core Function 2) • Governors regularly challenge the SLTs on the use and impact of pupil premium funding and question how disadvantaged children are being supported in school. (Core Function 3) This includes using the funding appropriately for more able pupils e.g. for music and drama lessons (Core Function 2) • In-school data shared termly, enables Governors to know about progress in English and Maths on a year group basis. (Core Function 2)

The practical impact activity record
Resource bank reference 83

One final suggestion for demonstrating impact is for governors to produce a termly or even an annual newsletter to parents. This has several functions. It identifies to parents who the members of the governing body are; it demonstrates the work and involvement of governors in the school, and it might encourage other parents to volunteer to become governors. We have not included a sample in our materials as they are so personal to the individual context of the school. If your governing body wishes to see some examples, many schools publish these on their school websites.

Classroom visits

Governors are volunteers, often with busy careers and outside obligations. It is, however, immensely useful, for all governors to have the opportunity to visit the school during the school day. These visits help governors develop their knowledge of the school. For some governors this might only be once a year; for others it might be more often. Parent governors have the perspective of their own children's experience of school and all these collective perspectives help the governing body, as a whole, to have a picture of the school.

There are two key points that we suggest school leaders highlight to governors prior to any visits.

"Occasional visits to schools enable governors to:

- ∞ *fulfil their statutory responsibility for the conduct of the school*
- ∞ *see whether the school is implementing their policies and improvement plans*
- ∞ *see how their policies and improvement plans are working in practice*

Individual governors do not have an automatic right to enter the school whenever they wish.

Focused governor monitoring visits should be:
- ∞ *in line with SIP priorities*
- ∞ *for an identified purpose linked to the governing body's responsibilities, such as safeguarding*
- ∞ *pre-arranged with the headteacher or executive headteacher*

It is not the governing body's role to assess teaching and learning or to interfere in the day-to-day running of the schools."

Classroom visits must always be arranged in advance and must have a clear focus.

They should follow an agreed protocol; for example, who will accompany the governor/s; whether or not a member of staff will be available to answer questions etc.

The key aim of visits is to help governors learn more about the school. If, at the end of a visit, a brief standard proforma is completed, as this can be used by all governors to increase their knowledge of the school.

Summary of activities, e.g. visiting classes; talking to staff and pupils; looking at resources	
What I have learned as a result of my visit	
Is there anything that I need clarifying or any questions I need answering before I report back to other Governors?	
What will I share with other Governors to help their knowledge of the school?	

Extract from the proforma for school visits by governors
Resource bank reference 85

Core function questions

Our final resource to support governing body training is a set of questions for governors to consider. These are arranged against each of the three core functions.

There are many such lists available on websites and in publications and our suggestion is that during a governing body training session, a brief question and answer session is held so that governors can discuss their responses to some of these.

Question / Aspect	Actions by Leaders	Impact / Difference
What role does the Board have in determining the strategic priorities for the school?		
How frequently are these priorities reviewed?		
What is the nature of collaborative relationships with other schools?		
What mechanisms does the Board employ to gain evidence of actions for improvement, other than via the Head Teacher?		
To what extent is there a culture of high expectations established at the school?		
How is the culture of ambition manifest by leaders, staff and pupils? How do governors know this?		
How is the distinctive character of the school determined, reviewed and maintained?		
To what extent are governors and leaders promoting fundamental British values? How do they know this?		
How effectively does the Board take decisions? Is there a clear delegation of operational matters to executive leaders?		
How well informed are governors about the school's safeguarding of pupils?		

1

Extract from a series of governor questions
Resource bank reference 86

✅ CASE-STUDY

'The Federation of Boldmere Schools has commissioned the services of Optimum Leadership Solutions (Nicki Bell) for several years to develop the strategic awareness of our Governing Board. Ensuring that all members of the Board are effective in meeting their three core areas when supporting and challenging the schools. All the training materials used and provided by Optimum Leadership Solutions help to provide our Board with a clear strategic steer of what they must do in their roles as governors.

This was evidenced in our most recent Ofsted inspection and referenced in our report as follows: Boldmere Infants Ofsted November 2023 – 'Leaders and governors are mindful of ensuring that the well-being of all staff is a priority. Staff feel valued and are proud to work here. Governors are skilled and committed. They understand their roles well and regularly visit the school to check the actions of leaders.'

All training materials used to professionally develop the roles of our governors are excellent and in line with the inspection framework and other statutory requirements. The training has been expertly facilitated by Nicki Bell and she also challenges our governors during her sessions to ensure that they are clear on what their roles in school are and how they can be developed in the future to meet the ever-changing needs of the educational landscape that we are faced with'.

Carl Glasgow
Executive Headteacher, The Boldmere Federation, Sutton Coldfield

'Just to say a huge thank you for yesterday. You gave us lots of clear, manageable ideas to help the governors move forward.
I think you pitched everything just right, so thanks for a great job and it was just what we needed!'

Headteacher of a Staffordshire Primary School November 2023

 # REFLECTIONS

∞ An effective governing body is of immense value to a school, but it is essential that every member of the governing body has a clear understanding of the role and understands the three core functions.
∞ Governor training needs to be revisited regularly but it can be difficult to arrange with governor commitments and time constraints. Having a set of resources in school enables the headteacher to deliver training which supports the governing body in becoming consistently effective.
∞ An annual cycle of skills audit; training plan; collation of impact, governing body improvement plan and scheduled school visits all helps governors to be able to develop their personal skills, knowledge, and effectiveness. It also gives the headteacher and senior leadership team confidence that the governors can talk, knowledgably about the school and its work.

 # RESOURCES

Resource 79
A PowerPoint presentation to support governor training.

Resource 80
Governor skills audit

Resource 81
Governor training plan

Resource 82
Sample governance improvement plan.

Resource 83
A practical activity to help the governing body demonstrate impact.

Resource 84
Protocols for classroom visits.

Resource 85
Pro-forma for classroom visits.

Resource 86
Core function questions.

Resource 87
Governing body file – organiser sheets.

Resource 88
Suggested contents for governance file.

 FURTHER READING

The key Department for Education documents for governing bodies are:

Maintained schools' governance guide
https://www.gov.uk/guidance/governance-in-maintained-schools

Academy trust governance guide
https://www.gov.uk/guidance/-governance-in-academy-trusts

To access **all the resources** in the **online resource bank** for a small one-off subscription just:

- ∞ email headshipmatters@proton.me or
- ∞ visit www.tinyurl.com/3vtzknpu or
- ∞ scan the QR code below

Communication and well-being matters

WHY

Our belief is that effective headteachers need many skills, but the ability to communicate with a wide range of audiences is vital. To be an impactful leader, you must be able to communicate effectively. Good communication is a core leadership skill and a characteristic of a good leader. Headteachers need to be skilled communicators at many levels and with a wide range of different audiences, from the youngest children; to colleagues; parents; governors, external professionals, peers, and the wider community. As headteachers we communicate in many ways – through writing, speaking, presenting, facilitating and through our actions as well as our words. In the 21st century, good communication skills include the ability to have excellent online skills and may encompass social media which also comes with its own myriad of challenges.

When planning a session on communication with several groups of headteachers recently, we found multiple lists of leadership skills.

One that we liked was an article by the International Institute for Management Development (IMD) which listed eight leadership strengths to develop, namely:

1. Self-awareness
2. Situational awareness
3. Excellent communication skills
4. Effective negotiation skills
5. Conflict resolution skills
6. Collaboration skills and intercultural sensitivity
7. Ability to work with different personal styles and approaches
8. Being able to make courageous or difficult decisions

Of these, most are based around effective communication. The full article is available on the imd.org website and is titled, "The eight best leadership strengths to focus on in 2023".

Your communication, as a headteacher needs to be purposeful and appropriate to the intended audience. You need to be able to clearly express ideas and share information. Effective communication helps to build trust and inspires and motivates others. Leaders who lack strong communication skills can be misunderstood thereby creating barriers and hampering positive relationships which, in turn, can impact upon the culture of the school. Clear communication supports school improvement as people understand what is required of them and are therefore able to engage positively with initiatives.

Verbal communication is perhaps the first mode of communication that we think of when considering our communication skills. We generally use spoken communication informally and written communication rather more formally. Spoken communication is more likely to encompass a relationship and will have a more emotional level with listeners than written communication. Spoken communication also has the benefit of being able to clear up misunderstandings immediately, based on feedback given by the listener. This results in a greater degree of certainty that the message was received. Written communication is also generally recorded for later retrieval, whereas spoken communication is generally not recorded. Good communication links with the area of emotional intelligence, (see building block one). Leaders can demonstrate empathy by being authentic and developing strong, active listening skills. Knowledge of emotional intelligence and the skill of self-management also provides an understanding of how to manage situations that may be stressful such as challenging conversations with colleagues or parents.

Our top tips for developing good communication include:

1. Be honest, sincere, and authentic.
2. Be accessible – so many headteachers tell us that they can prevent minor issues becoming major problems by talking to parents at the gate at the start or end of the school day.
3. Develop active listening skills, both in yourself and your staff. Active listening enables you to fully understand the issues and perspective of others which enables you to resolve situations.
4. Do your homework – when you know you have a potentially challenging conversation, make sure you know the context and be prepared.
5. Be aware of your body language – make it positive with eye contact, affirming gestures and show you are paying attention.
6. Ask well-constructed questions – good leaders listen more than they speak. Try to identify the key issues through your questioning.
7. Don't shy aware from difficult conversations – ignoring possible conflicts simply escalates situations.
8. Don't use educational acronyms with those who may not understand them.

 **HOW**

Conducting surveys to establish views and opinions

Parents - a generic survey

Parents and carers can be surveyed in different ways. It may happen informally, for example, on the playground, or formally through a written survey. We always aim to work in partnership with parents and by giving regular opportunities for feedback, it can help the school find out what it is doing well and where it could do better. Honest constructive feedback on how the school is meeting the needs of pupils is invaluable, although there will always be a few parents who, whatever is done, will not be happy. Building an annual whole-school survey into monitoring calendars ensures that this is a regular process. Our suggestion is to distribute this survey at the spring term parent interview meeting. This is a good time of year to collect useful data. The children are settled into their classes, and it is the halfway point in the year giving parents a good picture of the education that the child is receiving. It can either be done through a printed copy or electronically. Many schools give parents access to electronic devices during the usual wait-time at these events, so that they can input their responses immediately.

Schools may choose to ask any relevant questions and depending upon context, may have specific areas that they wish to explore such as assessment, SEND provision or aspects of the curriculum. One of the simplest solutions for a generic survey is to use the current Ofsted Parent View questions. Using this serves several purposes. Firstly, it is concise and deals with issues shared by all schools. Secondly, all schools benefit from having responses to questions that Ofsted will ask, well in advance of actual inspection. Finally, it gives parents the chance to think about the questions that will be asked at the time of inspection which may result in more carefully considered responses to Ofsted.

At the time of writing, the questions being asked are:

Ofsted Parent View questions https://parentview.ofsted.gov.uk
The survey asks parents to respond to fourteen statements and questions.

- ∞ My child is happy at this school.
- ∞ My child feels safe at this school.
- ∞ The school makes sure its pupils are well behaved.
- ∞ My child has been bullied and the school dealt with the bullying quickly and effectively.
- ∞ The school makes me aware of what my child will learn during the year.

- ∞ When I have raised concerns with the school they have been dealt with properly.
- ∞ Does your child have special educational needs and/or disabilities (SEND)? (yes/no)

    If yes, the survey asks parents how strongly they agree with this statement:

- ∞ 'My child has SEND, and the school gives them the support they need to succeed.'
- ∞ The school has high expectations for my child.
- ∞ My child does well at this school.
- ∞ The school lets me know how my child is doing.
- ∞ There is a good range of subjects available to my child at this school.
- ∞ My child can take part in clubs and activities at this school.
- ∞ The school supports my child's wider personal development.
- ∞ I would recommend this school to another parent. (yes or no)

Parents - a survey with a specific focus

There are times when it is useful to collect additional parental perspectives about the school. One such time is shortly after the new cohort of the youngest pupils have started at the school. This can be immensely useful in planning future induction programmes. A sample is included in our resource bank. Another time to ask parents and pupils about the school is shortly before pupils leave, usually at the end of key stage one or two.

Statement	Response		
The information that we received when we were choosing a school for our child was accurate.	Extremely clear and accurate.	We received most of the information we needed to make a choice.	We would have liked more information.
Once we were allocated a place at the school, we were given enough information to enable us to prepare our child for starting school.	Good information enabled us to prepare our child for school.	Appropriate information given.	We would have liked more information.
Our child enjoyed the induction visits to the school in the summer term.	Strongly agree	Agree	Our child found these difficult.
Having the first week of part-time school was helpful for our child.	Strongly agree	This was helpful for our child.	Our child did not need part-time sessions.

Extract from induction survey for parents
Resource bank reference 89

Staff

As with the generic parent survey, Ofsted also publish a staff survey which they use at the time of inspection. Once again, there are many good reasons for using these questions when carrying out a regular staff survey. The staff survey currently has twenty-three questions and asks staff to identify their role within the school e.g. senior leader, support staff etc., although this question can be left blank if staff are worried that they could be identified. The survey asks questions about a variety of issues including child safety, improvement since last inspection, behaviour management, professional development, school culture and workload.

(https://assets.publishing.service.gov.uk/media/5a81eaf8e5274a2e87 dc02ca/Staff_survey_questions_-_schools_-_January_2018.pdf

Pupils

One aspect of monitoring in schools is to talk to pupils, to gain their perspective through pupil voice activities. This would generally relate to talking to them about their work. There are also more informal opportunities to get the views of children.

Many schools have some kind of 'tea with me' activity on a regular basis when a small group of children meet with the headteacher to talk about other aspects of school life – for example, what they like and don't like about the school; favourite subjects; extra-curricular activities they might enjoy etc. The bonus for the pupils is usually that the meeting involves drinks of squash and biscuits!

Another valuable opportunity is gaining the perspective of pupils at specific times. In our resource bank, we include a Year 6 exit audit as an example. This example is a formal audit with tick boxes.

Statement	Response				
I have enjoyed being at this school	All the time	Most of the time	Some of the time	Almost never	Never
Teachers have helped me to do my best	In every lesson	In most lessons	In some lessons	In very few lessons	In none of my lessons
My teachers have given me work that has challenged me	In every lesson	In most lessons	In some lessons	In very few lessons	In none of my lessons
I have enjoyed learning at this school	All the time	Most of the time	Some of the time	Almost never	Never
Teachers listen to what I have to say in lessons	Strongly agree	Agree	Neither agree nor disagree	Disagree	Strongly disagree
There is an adult at school I can talk to if something is worrying me	Strongly agree	Agree	Neither agree nor disagree	Disagree	Strongly disagree

Extract from our Year 6 exit audit
Resource bank reference 90

Schools may also like to give pupils the chance to write their own thoughts around questions such as:

∞ "Tell me about your favourite times at the school and why you have enjoyed them?"
∞ "If you could change anything about being at our school, what would it be?"
∞ "What advice would you give to a future pupil at our school?"

Challenging conversations

'Relationships succeed or fail one conversation at a time.'
Susan Scott

At some points in our professional lives, we will encounter difficult situations when we must engage in a challenging conversation with a colleague, a parent, an external professional, or any number of other people.

Human nature means that many of us will try to avoid confrontation but sometimes it is inevitable, and having a strategy to help us plan for the conversation may help achieve an outcome that enables us to move forward.

Success (or failure) in the workplace depends largely upon the quality of relationships e.g. with children, colleagues and parents and these relationships are based on conversations.

When we work with headteachers and senior leaders, we often collate a list of the types of conversations that they dread. We ask colleagues to identify what these conversations may be about, why they dread them, and whether there are any common features or patterns within difficult conversations.

Dealing with "the difficult…"
The strategies/approaches/actions generated by practitioners.

Behaviour: **Those who are not willing to change practice…**

Strategies:
- Ask them what they would like to do – with the intention of sharing ideas
- Establish what motivates them – 'what would you like to do and why?'
- Share and show examples of what positive differences are possible
- Reference the real benefits for pupils – why would you not want to adopt this?
- Set out your clear expectations – by easing gently into writing lists for small steps to success
- Don't overwhelm them and don't criticize too much. Better to provide positive and developmental feedback to generate a 'feel good' factor in them.

Practitioner generated strategies for 'dealing with the difficult'
Resource bank reference 91

It is important to try to understand the causes of the challenging conversation. We try to look at the difficult conversation from the other person's perspective so that we can try to unpick why the person is behaving in a particular way and what outcome they want from the conversation.

Our advice to headteachers is that it is important to be politely assertive and there are steps to take to help with this. For example,

- Clarify your own thoughts and feelings about the situation.
- Understand that you have permission to speak.
- Express yourself clearly and speak directly to the other person.
- Make sure that you ascribe your feelings to yourself, don't apportion blame.
- Think through what outcomes you expect but don't assume you know how the other person will respond.
- Plan carefully for what you want to say.
- No-one else has a right to criticise you for this, providing you act professionally.
- Other people will normally value an honest well-considered idea.

- Avoid sarcasm, accusative statements, character assassination, or absolutes.
- Speak calmly and ask for clarification and confirmation.

As well as being a skilled communicator, headteachers are also responsible for ensuring that their staff have good communication skills. An exercise that we do with headteachers is to get them to discuss different scenarios to think about how they would improve the communication skills, verbal, written and non-verbal of their staff.

Scenarios for discussion about how you would improve the communication skills, (verbal, written, and non-verbal), of your staff.
1. **Confidentiality breach by a teacher:** You have just spent an hour with an angry parent who informs you that a teacher spoke to another parent at the end of the school day yesterday, and named her child and described an incident that she only found out about from her child yesterday evening. What do you do?
2. **Quality variation of written reports to parents:** Two siblings in school, one in Y2 and one in Y5. Reports go home and parents ask to speak with you the following day, regarding the variation in report content and style. One is detailed, accurate, bespoke, and informative. The other is bland, general, and short. How do you tackle the quality variation with the teacher?
3. **Staff room bickering:** Your office is next door to the staffroom, from where at lunch times you can hear bickering between two groups of staff. This is becoming more frequent and other staff are choosing not to go in there for their lunch. What do you do?
4. **Safeguarding:** One teacher "forgets" to record incidents onto CPOMS and when he does it is always a very brief entry. He tells you about the incidents and his concerns but doesn't always confirm it into the system. What do you do?

Sample of some real-life scenarios
Resource bank reference 92

Listening skills

We have referenced in other 'blocks' quotes from Stephen R. Covey and we feel that listening skills relate to his habit 5, "Seek first to understand, then to be understood."

"Many people do not listen with the intent to understand; they listen with the intent to reply". (Steven Covey 'The seven habits of highly effective people')

We recognise that communication is probably the most important skill in life. As a society, we spend a great deal of time teaching children to speak, read and write but don't really teach children to listen.

In conversations, we want to get our point or opinion across to listeners. Because of this motivation, we don't often listen carefully to the other person or people. We may pretend we are listening or selectively hear only parts of the conversation which may mean we miss the meaning. You listen to yourself as you prepare in your mind what you are going to say, the questions you are going to ask, etc. You filter everything you hear through your life experiences, your frame of reference. Consequently, you decide prematurely what the other person means before they finish communicating.

Active listening

When we think about communication, we are possibly thinking of talking rather than listening. How well you listen has a major impact on your leadership effectiveness and the quality of your relationships with others. Different studies suggest we only remember between 25% and 50% of what we hear, i.e. half of the conversation. If this is the case, then it is clearly a skill we should work to improve. Changes in technology, such as the mobile phone and social media mean that we are constantly distracted, and our listening skills may be suffering because of this.

Listening is not just hearing; it is an intense personal involvement with another person. It requires you to demonstrate your commitment to listening by using appropriate body language e.g. eye contact; appropriate facial expressions; not interrupting or diverting and not thinking up your response while the other person is talking. If you listen carefully then you can clarify, summarise, and demonstrate that you have understood. Summarising is a key test of listening – you cannot summarize if you haven't listened.

The way to improve your listening skills is to develop your skill of active listening. Making a conscious effort to hear not only the words that another person is saying but the complete message being communicated. To do this, you must pay attention to the other person very carefully. You cannot allow yourself to become distracted by whatever else may be going on around you, or by thinking of your response while the other person is still speaking.

You need to concentrate and not allow yourself to get bored and lose focus on what the other person is saying.

There are simple ways to demonstrate that you are listening, for example by nodding, smiling, offering the occasional question or comment and by looking at the speaker directly.

Examples of behaviours that will inhibit the speaker would be interrupting them; mentally preparing your response being distracted by environmental factors and demonstrating negative body language i.e. looking bored.

We work with headteachers to give them some strategies to develop active listening in their schools. One that they enjoy is the back-to-back activity, where two people sit facing opposite directions. One has a card on which there is a simple line-drawn picture. Person one must describe the picture accurately, using only line, angle, and length descriptions, not "just draw a flower or star". Person two attempts to draw it by following the instructions from person one. The results can be interesting! Within our resource bank there are samples to use for this activity as well as suggestions for some other listening skills activities for both staff and children.

We would also strongly recommend explicitly developed listening skills with pupils. A resource book that we have round very helpful is "Teaching children to listen" by Liz Spooner and Jacqui Woodcock, containing a huge number of activities to develop these essential skills.

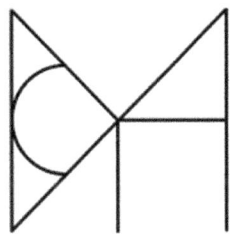

Set of pictures at resource bank reference 96

Body language

Communication is about so much more than words. When verbal and non-verbal cues contradict one another, people receiving the message tend to believe the non-verbal communication. This is because people communicate non-verbal messages even when they consciously try to avoid doing this. Non-verbal communication reveals a lot about you as a communicator and how you relate to other people. Those skilled at interpreting body language suggest that there are distinguishable cues from the way eyes move during conversations, for example, looking left and up indicates the person is recalling a visual memory. We are not suggesting this level of understanding is necessary, but as a headteacher you need to be aware of some of the messages you may inadvertently be giving such as facial expression, posture, gestures, and eye contact.

Albert Mehrabian's work about spoken communication generated this diagram, which is widely quoted in articles about non-verbal communication. This indicates that when non-verbal signals conflict with the verbal content, the words carry only 7% of the message; the tone of voice 38%, but the body language a huge 55%.

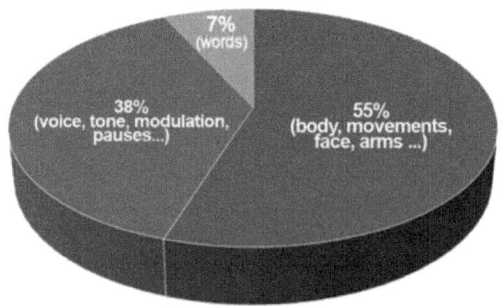

The experiments that resulted in this model related to communication of feelings and attitudes. That means that these figures will not apply in every work situation involving communication, but if feelings and attitudes are involved, such as when having a challenging conversation, this is worth considering, (resource bank reference 97).

Surviving and thriving as a headteacher

Our regular work with headteachers gives us an understanding of both the joys, but also some of the pressures of the role in the 21st century. Headteachers are sometimes expected both by colleagues and, to some extent, by society, to be "heads of answers". Headship can be a lonely place – always supporting colleagues but sometimes with no personal support network. A recent survey reported that 76% of education professionals reported work being a contributing factor in their symptoms of negative well-being. It is imperative that headteachers recognise that they matter and their own emotional well-being and mental health matters too. One of the first priorities for every headteacher must be to develop strategies to look after yourself and your own well-being. Attending to your own psychological and emotional needs is not selfish. It demonstrates commitment and courage to be proactive about being the best version of yourself, so that you can serve others.

There are many blogs on social media about surviving and thriving as a headteacher. We collated strategies from some of these into a checklist:

1. Recognise that you are a not a super-hero!
2. Realise that whilst that the show must go on, you don't always have to be there to lead it.
3. Make sure that you engage with a community - essential for good mental health – you need to attach yourself to a professional group of like-minded people.
4. Learn to switch off and say "no"- a long term behavioural change.
5. Be kind to yourself.
6. Remain connected to your values.
7. Get clarity on your professional vision – what do you want for your school?
8. Acknowledge that the role is tough.
9. Look after yourself.

Of these, one that we feel is essential is having a personal professional network of people that you can call on to talk things through, seek advice from or just have a moan to. One of the reasons for the feeling of isolation in headship is that some people feel that they should innately know how to do the job and that to seek help and support is to show weakness.

When we are feeling calm and rational, we recognise that this is not true. Everyone needs help at some point and peer support groups or simply a colleague in a similar role can ease the pressure.

We know that one of the main reasons that our termly headteacher groups have continued to meet, over many years, is that along with some professional development that we provide, there is also plenty of time to chat, share experiences, ask for support, and relax in a non-judgmental safe space.

A wise friend once said that "life is a cake and work is a slice". As a headteacher, the work slice can sometimes be far too big. However, recognizing that you have a life beyond the school is important to keep things in perspective. Your identity is more than your job. The advice from psychologists is to create balance in your life by dedicating time to yourself, to the things that bring you joy, to your family and friends.

Easily said, but heartfelt advice from the two of us who can now see the realities of headship from a different perspective.

We have found several articles online about well-being. One that we felt useful to share was the NHS '5 steps to mental well-being' https://www.nhs.uk/mental-health/self-help/guides-tools-and-activities/five-steps-to-mental-wellbeing/

We include the document in the resource bank, (reference 98). In a nutshell it says:

1. Connect with other people - good relationships are important for your mental wellbeing.
2. Be physically active - being active is not only great for your physical health and fitness. Evidence also shows it can also improve your mental wellbeing.
3. Learn new skills - research shows that learning new skills can also improve your mental wellbeing by boosting self-confidence and raising self-esteem.
4. Give to others - research suggests that acts of giving and kindness can help improve your mental wellbeing by creating positive feelings and a sense of reward, thereby giving you a feeling of purpose and self-worth.
5. Pay attention to the present moment (mindfulness) - paying more attention to the present moment can improve your mental wellbeing. Some people call this awareness "mindfulness". Mindfulness can help you enjoy life more and understand

yourself better. It can positively change the way you feel about life and how you approach challenges.

CASE-STUDY

'I have attended Nicki and Alistair's headteacher professional development programme, (three full days per year), for my entire headship career, some ten years, to date. Why do I keep going back? Several reasons, not least of which is the consistently excellent level and range of professional development they provide for the group. But also because of the strong, mutually beneficial networking support and challenge each group member provides for one another.

In the early days Nicki and Alistair would always prompt us to agree protocols and agreed ways of working. But such is the embedded level of professional trust that we no longer require such formalities. I travel 75 miles for this each term and am fortunate to be part of a group well outside my geographical area. The group is comprised of headteachers from a wide range of local authorities, and with a range of experience.

I look forward so much to each day because I know I am in great company and there is plenty of time for discussion and problem solving. I come away with enhanced knowledge, with things I can use in school with my staff, but mostly knowing I have helped a fellow headteacher and in turn have been helped by a trusted colleague.
In addition, we have an active WhatsApp group for maintaining contact outside of the three face-to-face training days and we also hold social events too.

Such is the positive and mutual support that without this I probably wouldn't have been as effective as a headteacher as I believe I can be'.

Anonymous headteacher

REFLECTIONS

∞ Effective leaders need to have high level communication skills.

∞ Communication skills can be developed, and it is important that headteachers also develop these in their teams.

∞ One of the hardest parts of the role of leader is having challenging conversations. These are more successful when we plan for them and are aware of strategies to use.

∞ To survive and thrive as a headteacher, it is important to look after yourself. The isolation of the role means it is essential to build and maintain a professional support network and to look after yourself.

RESOURCES

Resource 89
Sample parent survey for YR first term induction.

Resource 90
Sample pupil survey for Y6 exit.

Resource 91
Dealing with the difficult – strategies created by practitioners.

Resource 92
Scenarios for improving communication skills of staff.

Resource 93
National College seven steps for fierce conversations.

Resource 94
Managing difficult conversations think piece.

Resource 95
Active listening think piece.

Resource 96
Back-to-back listening skills game pictures.

Resource 97
Body language pictures.

Resource 98
NHS '5 steps to mental well-being'.

 **FURTHER READING**

Liz Spooner and Jacqui Woodcock "Teaching children to listen in primary schools" Bloomsbury publishing, 2019.

Professor Toby Salt, "The Juggling Act: How to juggle leadership and life" John Catt publishing 2021

To access **all the resources** in the **online resource bank** for a small one-off subscription just:
- ∞ email headshipmatters@proton.me or
- ∞ visit www.tinyurl.com/3vtzknpu or
- ∞ scan the QR code below

Building Block **9**

Using and applying theory

 **WHY**

We have worked, for many years, with headteachers and their staff, always trying to help make their professional lives a little easier. We listen to their concerns and endeavour, where possible, to help them address these.

We are fully aware of how little time headteachers have to keep abreast of the mass of information, publications and new trends in the education world. One way in which we try to help is to access some of this and make our own interpretation of it which we can then share with participants on our training courses and through our own resources. Our interpretation of material is always from a practical, former headteacher perspective and not from an academic one. The internet enables anyone to find more in-depth and academic analyses of different elements of theory, should they wish to do so.

During our careers outside of schools, we have both worked to support the development of national resources, primarily when working as external consultants with the National College for School Leadership. We recognised, in our own professional lives, the need to have a grasp of some of the theory behind our practice. We know that many headteachers are proactive and instinctively find solutions to problems, for example, managing time and leading change initiatives.

Our belief is, that recognising that there is a research theory behind some of these actions, validates and deepens our ability to apply theory to our practice, and, in many cases, this makes the headteacher role easier.

This building block is therefore an overview of some of the theoretical models that we regularly use with headteachers and senior leaders. There are many others that we use, but we wanted to provide a taster to show how we use and adapt resources to support school leaders.

 HOW

Leading change

Headteachers spend a great deal of time evaluating the things that are going well and the things that need improving in their schools. They do this through the self-evaluation and school improvement processes supported by the monitoring programme – all outlined in the foundation stones chapter at the beginning of this book.

Having identified the aspects that need to change, the challenge is to lead that change successfully.

Professor John Kotter says, "Leadership is very much related to change. As the pace of change accelerates, there is naturally a great need for effective leadership." For some, change may cause anxiety, and therefore needs careful and skilled leadership. People often resist change because they are unsure of what is required of them. There are many reasons why intended changes fail.

Kotter gives several reasons:

∞ Complacency
∞ Failing to create teams with enough power to lead the change.
∞ Underestimating the power of vision.
∞ Failing to communicate the vision.
∞ Allowing obstacles, real or imagined, to block the vision.
∞ Failing to create short-term gains.
∞ Declaring victory too soon.
∞ Neglecting to embed the changes in the culture.
∞ Failure to consult.

Adapted from John P Kotter, "Leading Change" 1996.

Some years ago, we were both involved in delivering an initiative called 'The National Remodelling Programme'. One of the more useful things we retained from this programme was a straight-forward change equation that we have used frequently with school leaders at all levels. The original concept was created by Knoster who identified five different elements that need to be present for success when navigating a complex change or challenge. Knoster's full model and explanation is accessible on multiple websites. (The Knoster Model for complex change management, resource bank reference 99).

The model we use and apply to our action planning process, takes three of these elements:

∞ A compelling reason for change.   (R)
∞ A clear vision of the future.   (V)
∞ A coherent plan for getting there.   (P)

Therefore, $R + V + P = C$ where C is successful and sustainable change.

If there is no REASON, then there is resistance.
If there is no VISION, then there is confusion.
If there is no ACTION PLAN, then there is anxiety.

Our interpretation of this model is that headteachers should only initiate change if they can identify the compelling reason for it. A compelling reason is not something they have simply read about or have a vague understanding of. A compelling reason might be that outcomes in reading are falling and we require a change in reading resources or further training. The compelling reason must be clear to everyone – why we are spending time and energy on this initiative.

Leaders also need to have a clear vision of what they are aiming to achieve – their clear vision of the future i.e. what the change will deliver when achieved, for example, in this case, better outcomes in reading. Unless this vision is clearly articulated to everyone involved in implementing the change, it is unlikely to work.

The third element in our adapted model is the need for a clear action plan, for example:

- ∞ What will be completed?
- ∞ How will it be achieved?
- ∞ Who will lead and who will support?
- ∞ When will this happen – milestones are useful?
- ∞ What is the cost?

When colleagues know what is expected of them, they are more able to engage with the change. Richard Boyatzis said that without a clear plan of action, a change is only 5% likely to succeed, however, with a clear plan of action, it is 60% likely to succeed.

One other resource we frequently refer to in training when discussing change, is Fisher's personal transition curve, created by John Fisher in 2012. As with most of our theoretical models, this can be accessed on multiple sites online.

The message from this model is that there are many different emotional states that we experience when going through a change. Applying this to a school context, having identified that reading attainment is dipping, there is a phase of anxiety about making a change. This is followed by a feeling of happiness, that a change is going to happen.

The next phase is one of fear – "what have I started?" and "can I really do this?" – this is a time of self-doubt for a leader, and this is the point when some people give up and abandon the change. After the dip, things start to improve as the change gradually embeds and starts to work. This is a normal and natural process, and it helps, when initiating a change, to know you may experience some low points. The process clearly only goes through the transition curve if the change is compelling, with a clear vision and action plan as detailed above.

The learning cycle and Rosenshine's ten principles of instruction

One area of education research that has been hugely important in recent years has been the rapid growth of research evidence into how pupils learn and how practising teachers can use this research to maximise their teaching effectiveness. There is now an expectation that teachers engage in evidence-informed practice.

One example is the government investment of millions of pounds into research by the Education Endowment Foundation (EEF) which produces research reports for teachers to access and rates these in terms of their cost, evidence strength and impact on learning. The intention is that teachers engage with research and use it to adapt to their own schools and contexts.

There are also huge numbers of books and online articles published looking into metacognition and pedagogy. Many Early Career Teachers (ECT) have aspects of this work embedded into their on-going training and are bringing new ideas into their schools.

One publication that we have found helpful, due to the straight-forward language and models is "The fundamentals of teaching" by Mike Bell (Routledge 2021). The author has taken five key sources of evidence, namely, the EEF; John Hattie; Ceri Dean; the International Academy of Education (IAE) and the Institute for Education Sciences (IES) and recognised the parallels between the different sources.

Using this information, Bell has created a five-step model of a learning cycle, (Bell, p.22), which we have used extensively with our headteacher groups.

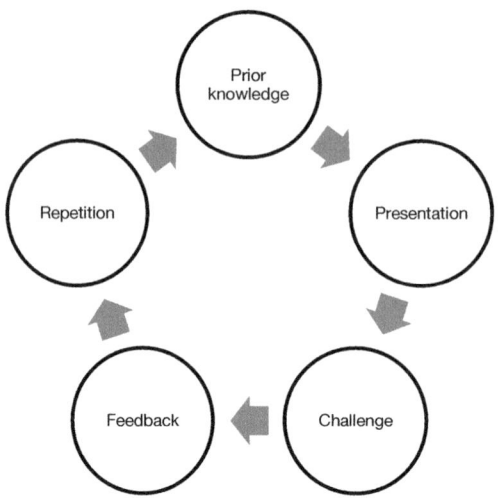

Mike Bell's learning cycle
Resource bank reference 101

We were already aware of the work of Barack Rosenshine and his ten research-based principles of instruction (American Educator, spring 2012). Rosenshine's work is referenced in Bell's book through his work with the International Academy of Education. We have been using these principles with school leaders for several years. The reference book that we always recommend for initial early reading of this work is "Rosenshine's principles in action" by Tom Sherrington. (John Catt Educational Ltd, 2019)

One of the practical ways in which we have applied some of our emerging understanding of the work on evidence-informed practice, is to build upon our tools for monitoring the quality of education and teacher effectiveness by creating a grid to incorporate Rosenshine's principles. Our logic in creating this was that our building block three relates to the quality of teaching over time. The wealth of materials in our online resource for this building block are intended, as the title suggests, to be used over an extended time frame.

Headteachers and senior leaders would not be monitoring all the areas at the same time. Rosenshine's principles, however, can be used in a single lesson. The full model for this resource is contained within our online resource bank, reference 103.

Monitoring of the application of Rosenshine's Principles of Instruction.

Ref	Question / Aspect	Minimal evidence	Developing use of the principles	Effective use of the principles
1	**Review at the start of the lesson** *This helps children access the prior knowledge and retrieve existing knowledge from long-term memory. This could include quizzing, summarising, recalling etc.*	Lesson starts with no reference to previous learning and no opportunities for children to engage in any recall.	Teacher starts lesson with a short review of previous learning by asking questions and checking for earlier misconceptions	Teacher starts lesson with a short class conversation about previously learned concepts and information, e.g. 'what was the main thing we learned in our maths lesson yesterday' or a range of activities such as brainstorming, paired recall – who can tell their partner two things about the story we read yesterday? or techniques such as using an example of previous work on a visualiser. References to active working walls can also help review.
2	**Present new material in small steps.** *This helps children avoid cognitive overload and helps them to process the information more effectively in their working memory.*	The teacher tells the children what they are going to do in the whole lesson. No attempt to break the tasks down. As a result, periodically throughout the lesson, all learning stops as the teacher needs to repeat the tasks.	Some tasks are broken down, but the steps are not small enough resulting in the children becoming overloaded and needing to seek reassurance and repetition of instructions during the lesson. This slows the lesson and the learning process.	The new material is presented in small steps in a logical sequence that children can hold in their working memory. The next step is not introduced until the first one has been mastered so learning is cumulative. For example, if teaching the punctuation of direct speech, introduce just one rule first e.g. where to position speech marks. Once this is mastered, the next step might be to start the speech with a capital letter. After each step, time is allowed for consolidation and checking for misconceptions.
3	**Ask lots of good questions** *Is there a variety of question styles/strategies e.g. recall, comprehension, application, synthesis, evaluation etc (Bloom's taxonomy) Questions help children practise new information and connect new and prior learning which helps retention and understanding.*	Few questions asked and these don't relate well to new information or prior learning. Questions are not differentiated by ability; hands up is a key strategy for response, many questions are closed.	Teacher uses some questioning strategies – include talk partners and some cold calling, but quality of the questions is not strong i.e. mostly knowledge and comprehension and mostly closed questions.	A wide range of questioning strategies – 'say it again better' 'think, pair, share', cold calling techniques, no opt-out, use of whiteboards etc. Teacher probes for depth and clarification in responses. Questioning techniques are used by the teacher to assess how well children have understood new information. Questions are both factual (knowledge and comprehension) and process (application, analysis etc) Children are confident and resilient in responding even if unsure of the answer.

Lesson observation proforma using Rosenshine's principles
Resource bank reference 103

Finally, in this section, we offer a simple model of learning that we created and use regularly that encompasses some of the work on learning.

Within our online resource bank, there is a scripted PowerPoint presentation, that uses this model and links it to our work on effective teaching – see resource bank reference 104.

'Learning can be defined as an alteration in long-term memory. If nothing has altered in long-term memory, nothing has been learned. However, pupils learn by connecting new knowledge with existing knowledge. Pupils also need to develop fluency and unconsciously apply their knowledge as skills. This must not be reduced to, or confused with, simply memorising disconnected facts. When inspectors evaluate the impact of the education provided by the school, their focus will primarily be on what pupils have learned.' Ofsted, SIH January 2024 para: 246

Defined end point

Logical progression/sequence of new knowledge and skills – small steps.
Build connections to deepen understanding
Ask lots of questions to support connections between new materials and prior learning retrieval practice.
Provide models and examples

Prior knowledge – assessed through short review of prior learning – establish connections

'Over the course of study, teaching is designed to help pupils to remember long-term, the content they have been taught and to integrate new knowledge into larger ideas.' SIH January 2024, in 'good' descriptor for QoE implementation, para: 454 bullet point 9

Spiral model of learning
Resource bank reference 105

Managing time

When working with headteachers and senior leaders, we have frequently referenced the work of Stephen R. Covey and his seminal work "The seven habits of highly effective people". (Simon & Schuster UK Ltd 1999). We believe that these are entirely relatable to school leadership, and we would recommend that school leaders find a precis of the book – there are many available online – to see what they might glean from the seven habits.

Covey's third habit of putting first things first provides an excellent model that may support headteachers in improving their time management. When we ask them about their biggest challenges, not having enough time is always high on their list of concerns. The modern world with 24/7 access to emails, mobile phones and social media seems, from our perspective, to be making this challenge even more difficult to manage.

Covey offers a time management matrix and suggests that leaders of high performing organisations spend 65-80% of their time in the important but not urgent quadrant and as little as 15% of their time in the urgent but not important quadrant. Leaders of less successful organisations reverse these time allocations. We include a few examples that he puts into each sector.

	Urgent	Not urgent
Important	Crises Deadlines	Planning Relationship building
Not important	Interruptions Some meetings	Trivia Some phone calls

We then thought about how this applied to headteachers and senior leaders and adapted the model.

	Urgent	Not urgent
Important	Child protection Angry parent	Planning, preparing policies, research, thinking time, major projects
Not important	Ad-hoc interruptions Finding solutions for others	Over-production Unnecessary 'tidying'

∞ We describe the urgent and important quadrant as where leaders must be reactive – the issue needs addressing immediately and cannot wait or be planned for.

∞ The important but not yet urgent quadrant is the important one. Issues here are currently not urgent, but if they are not addressed, they may become urgent. This is where leaders need to be proactive – this is the area of real strategic leadership.

∞ The urgent but not important quadrant is the area in which leaders who are seen as 'head of answers' often find themselves spending excessive time. This is a hard area to reduce, but effective leaders must be aware of how much time they spend on finding solutions for people who should really be able to find them for themselves.

∞ The not urgent and not important quadrant is not necessarily a waste of time but needs to be managed. A classroom example of this described to us was of a teacher who had created an excellent display about outer space with dark blue backing paper. Late on a Friday afternoon, the teacher was seen to be replacing the entire display with black backing paper. Was this an effective use of time?

Our suggestion when working with headteachers, is to create an empty grid and audit, over a day or longer, where they are spending their time – this is a simple, but often illuminating exercise that can help. There is a version of this in our online resource bank together with a second proforma to analyse the use of time, (resource bank reference 107).

Day in the life template

Core activities and codes A: Admin R: Routine job tasks e.g. leading assembly, being on gate I: Interruptions E: Overseeing quality of education e.g. monitoring S: Strategic work e.g. school improvement; futures planning M: Meetings C: Coaching/supporting colleagues P: Time with children O: Other (describe)		Urgent	Not urgent
	important	QUADRANT 1	QUADRANT 2
	Not important	QUADRANT 3	QUADRANT 4

1 and 2 below are examples.

Activity number for reference	Time	Duration in minutes	Core activity	Urgent Tick if task was urgent.	Important Tick if task was important
1	8.45am	15 mins	R – on gate welcoming children		√
2	9.00	15 mins	M – meeting with irate parent	√	√
1					
2					
3					
4					

A 'day in the life' template
Resource bank reference 106

Effective questioning

Within Rosenshine's ten principles of instruction, his third principle relates to the quality of questioning – one of the key elements of highly effective teaching.

Effective questioning underpins retrieval to establish prior learning; the presenting of new learning; the making of connections between new and prior learning; the processing and reviewing of new learning; the checking for misconceptions and the review of learning process. Questioning also underpins many aspects of the assessment process.

The ability to create and deliver well-constructed questions and to have strong questioning techniques and strategies are integral to every classroom and essential to every teacher's pedagogical repertoire. The questions a teacher asks and the strategies they deploy, can make a significant difference to the quality of teaching and learning.

Through effective questioning, we require active engagement from all pupils in lessons; we support pupils to develop the ability to ask questions themselves i.e. to have enquiring minds; we challenge thinking; probe for meaning and develop thinking skills.

We accept that questioning is a crucial pedagogical skill, but we may not always support our teachers in developing this, either in initial training or once qualified. We need to ensure that all our teachers use questions well to improve the quality of both teaching and learning. We need to monitor this to ensure that teachers questioning is not dominated by closed, low level questions which make little cognitive demand of pupils, but equally, provide minimal learning opportunities.

This is not to say that closed questions are unimportant – they can be useful in knowledge retrieval and can help less confident pupils by giving them confidence to respond. The skill of the teacher is to use different types of questions that focus on learning and give the opportunity to differentiate to meet different needs.

There are many classification taxonomies to guide teacher questioning but the simplest and probably most well-known framework, that from experience, works in the primary classroom is Bloom's cognitive taxonomy (1956), later revised by Anderson and Krathwohl (2001). The revisions were made to incorporate new knowledge and thought into the framework to link better to our growing understanding of how children develop and learn and how teachers plan for, then teach and subsequently assess their pupils. From the perspective of a primary teacher, the revisions don't impact hugely on the use of the taxonomy, so we have focussed on the original classifications as there is more support material for these than for the revisions.

The framework provides a useful structure to scaffold our ability to ask questions at different levels of cognitive complexity. The taxonomy classifies educational objectives into six groups according to their level of complexity and outlines the kind of thinking that is required to meet the objective. Ideally teachers should combine questions that require 'lower-order thinking', (often closed questions), to assess knowledge and comprehension and questions that require high-order thinking, (often open questions), to assess pupils' abilities to apply; analyse; synthesise and evaluate.

Bloom's taxonomy assumes that the objectives are hierarchical, starting with knowledge and going thorough to evaluation. It is necessary to start at the first stage and move through the levels in order to gain higher order thinking skills i.e. children need to acquire knowledge before they can understand it or apply it to a new situation.

Classification	Some possible sentence starters
Knowledge	What is…? How is…? Where is…? How did…? List 3…. Which one…? Can you recall…?
Comprehension	Why didn't…? Can you explain…? What facts show…? What is meant…? What can you say about…? How would you summarise…?
Application	How would you use…? What examples…? What questions would you ask…? How would you show your understanding of…?
Analysis	How would you react…? Why do you think…? What evidence can you find…? How would you classify? What inference can you make …?
Synthesis	How would you improve…? How could you change…? What happened before…? How would you test…? How would you adapt…?
Evaluation	Do you agree with the actions of…? What would you recommend…? What choice would you have made…? How would you prove/disprove…?

Teachers use questions to promote pupils' thinking. We endeavour to ask different kinds of questions often at different levels of difficulty and we attempt to differentiate our questioning to challenge children at an appropriate level. We use 'closed' questions – those with a limited number of correct answers, and 'open' questions – those which prompt multiple answers.

Research evidence suggests that effective teachers use a greater number of open questions than less-effective teachers. The mix of open and closed questions will, of course, depend on what is being taught and the objectives of the lesson. However, teachers who don't ask open questions in a lesson may be providing insufficient cognitive challenge for pupils.

We should plan some of our questions to ensure that they are linked to the lesson objectives and to pupil outcomes. This is not the same as scripting a lesson as that would prevent flexibility and responsiveness to pupils, but thinking about our questioning whilst lesson planning enables us to use the skill of questioning effectively.

One issue for teachers is that they often only ask questions that relate to the first two levels i.e. knowledge and comprehension. Around 60 per cent of questions expect only factual information from students *(Lee and Kinzie, 2012)*. By remaining at these two levels pupils are not always challenged; they are not required to develop higher order thinking skills as the questions they are asked do not required them to use the skills of application; analysis; synthesis and evaluation. Low-level questioning aimed at recall and basic comprehension will plateau classroom learning quickly. Higher-level questions can produce deeper learning and thinking, but there needs to be a balance, both have a place, and a mixture of questions is recommended.

Our aim is to support teachers in developing their use of these higher-level questioning techniques to improve learning of their pupils.

In our online resource bank, there are many resources including a PowerPoint presentation, reference 108 and an audit proforma to support monitoring the quality of questioning, reference 109. There are also two think pieces on effective questioning techniques reference 110 and the importance of effective questioning, reference 111.

⚙️ CASE-STUDY

'As part of our professional growth plan at Thomas Russell Junior School, we invited Nicki in to do a staff training session about metacognition, questioning and building long-term memory. This followed a day with the senior leadership team in the autumn term to update our SEF and confirm the key areas of the school improvement plan.

As always, Nicki brings a huge amount of experience, insight, and common sense into what makes effective teaching and learning. Always extremely well prepared, she covered a huge amount of ground in a very accessible format.

The training made perfect sense to us and teachers and teaching assistants alike thoroughly enjoyed the training and found it very informative. We are now trialling various aspects of the training to see how it works in practice for us.

We are looking forward to welcoming Nicki back later in the term to give us some feedback on our journey. Our aim is to be the most effective leaders of learning we can be, and Nicki is an integral part of the process.'

James Emery
Headteacher, Thomas Russell Junior School, Staffordshire.

👤💬 REFLECTIONS

∞ Understanding the theory underpinning your work in school gives you confidence in your actions and helps articulate the rationale behind your actions.
∞ There is a wealth of material available, and you can't, and don't need to access it all. Talking with professional colleagues and

signposting one another to useful material is often the best way to find what you need.

∞ We have highlighted just four areas that we find particularly useful when working with headteachers and senior leaders; leading change; the learning cycle; managing time and effective questioning. We selected these because they are the areas we are most often asked to support leaders with. We have simply accessed some published resources and adapted them to meet the needs of our colleagues. We hope they might help you.

 # RESOURCES

Resource 99
The Knoster model of successful change.

Resource 100
Fisher's personal transition curve.

Resource 101
Learning cycle – adapted from Mike Bell model.

Resource 102
Information sheet on the Rosenshine principles of instruction.

Resource 103
Lesson observation proforma using Rosenshine's principles of instruction.

Resource 104
A PowerPoint presentation on 'high quality teaching and learning'.

Resource 105
Spiral model of learning.

Resource 106
A day in the life proforma.

Resource 107
Analysis of the day in the life time matrix.

Resource 108
A PowerPoint presentation on effective questioning.

Resource 109
An audit of classroom questioning.

Resource 110
Effective questioning techniques think piece.

Resource 111
The importance of effective questioning notes.

Resource 112
Bloom's taxonomy vocabulary.

 # FURTHER READING

John Kotter, "Our iceberg is melting", Macmillan 2006
Stephen Covey, "The seven habits of highly effective people" Simon & Schuster

Mike Bell, "The fundamentals of teaching" Routledge 2021
Tom Sherrington, "Rosenshine's principles in action" John Catt 2019
Sherrington & Caviglioli, "The Teaching Walkthrus series" John Catt 2020

Busch and Watson, "The science of learning", Routledge 2019

Darren Mead, "The expert teacher", Independent Thinking Press 2019

Mike Gershon, "How to use questioning in the classroom", 2013

Kate Jones, "Retrieval practice books 1 and 2" - John Catt 2019

To access **all the resources** in the **online resource bank** for a small one-off subscription just:

- ∞ email headshipmatters@proton.me or
- ∞ visit www.tinyurl.com/3vtzknpu or
- ∞ scan the QR code below